The Art of Crystal Grid Making

Insights, Ideas, and Beautiful Photos to Inspire!

Copyright © 2018 Tiari

ISBN: 0-692-05060-4

ISBN-13: 978-0-692-05060-6

All rights reserved. No part of this book may be reproduced, stored in a retrieval system, or transmitted in any form by any means electronic, mechanical, photocopy, recording—other than for "fair use" as brief quotations embodied in articles or reviews with proper references to the book and author—without the expressed written consent of the author.

The author of this book does not dispense medical advice or other professional advice or prescribe the use of any technique as a form of diagnosis or treatment for any physical, medical or emotional condition.

Mention of any specific companies, organizations, authorities or individuals in this book does not imply endorsement by the author or the publisher, nor does it imply they offer endorsement of this book or its author or publisher

Dedicated to those who appreciate the beauty and power of the living crystal. Giving thanks to my wonderful husband and daughter for their help and support with the creation of this book. Giving thanks to those who put their crystals into Divine service for the greatest good of all. And so it is. ~ from the heart

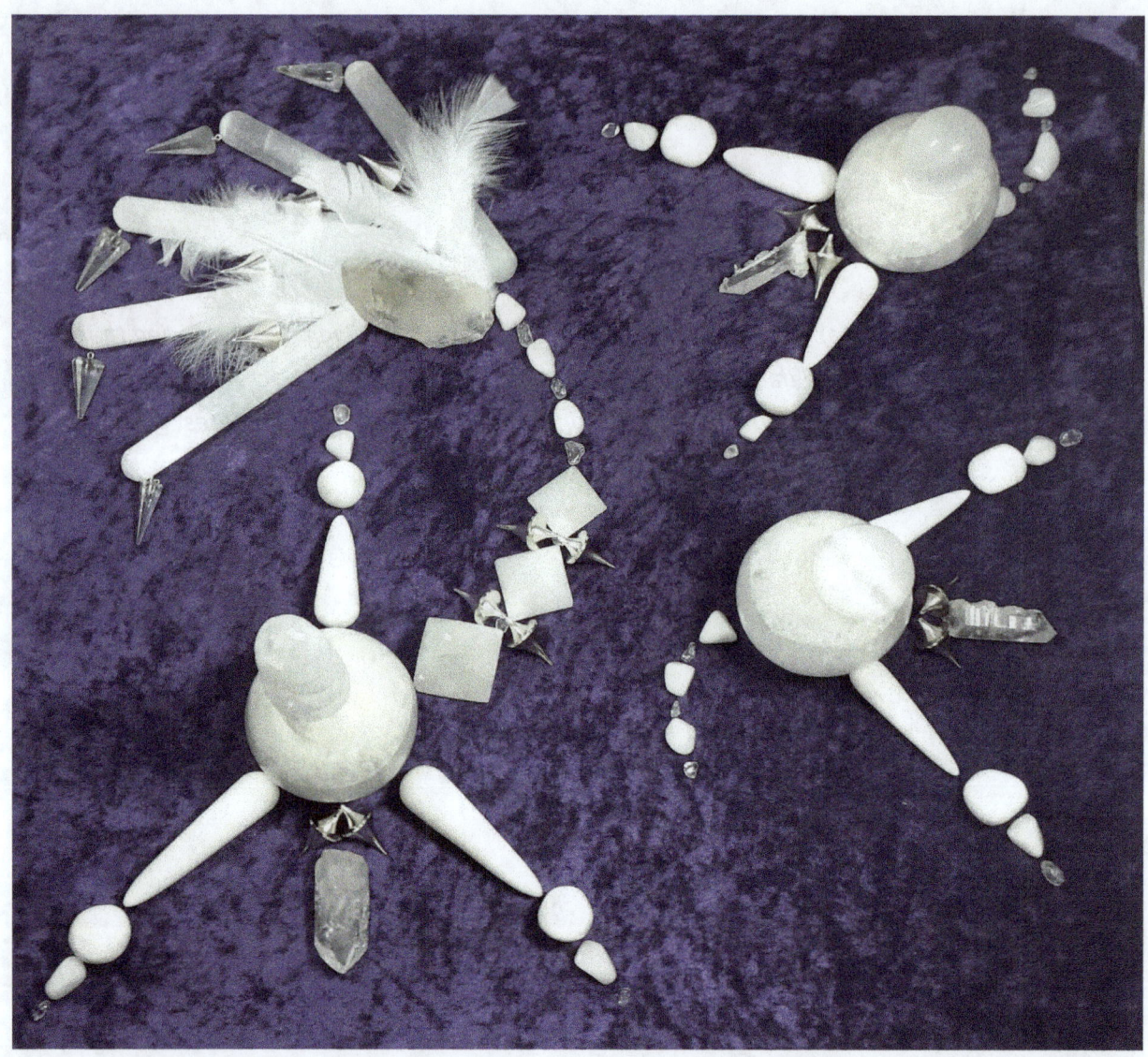

"Galactic Flight" Scolecite wands and tumbleds, Selenite wands, spheres, pyramids and standing spirals, Stellar Beam Calcite, Arkansas Lemurian Seed Quartz, White Calcite tumbleds, Clear Quartz and Silver pendulums, with white feathers. The name came about after it was created for the white photo in the governing colors guide. I recreated it on the deep purple to see it with contrast and it had me feeling like I was on a galactic flight.

CONTENTS

Author's Note

Introduction I-V

CHAPTER 1 What is a Crystal Grid? 1

CHAPTER 2 The Living Power of a Crystal 7

CHAPTER 3 Common Questions 13

    Can I create a grid to include more than just one affirmation? 13

    Do I need a layout board? 13

    Will my grids still work if I forget to cleanse the energy of my crystals between uses? 14

    How long do I have to keep the grid in place for? 15

    What are good crystals to start with? 15

    Are there crystals and stones that do not combine well together and how would I know? 16

    What is the difference between an alchemy grid and simply an artfully arranged collection of crystals and other materials? 17

    I like to make crystal gardens. Are they crystal alchemy grids? 18

    How does this art put my crystals into Divine service? 19

CHAPTER 4 Elements of Creating Alchemically 21

    Gratitude Affirmation 21

    Clean Energy 23

Cleansing is Charging   25

Layout Board or Undisturbed Space   25

Crystals, Stones, and Metals   26

Frequency Field Stabilizers   27

Power Generators and Program Directing Crystals   28

Sacred Geometry and Symbols   29

Grid Templates and Free Form Designs   30

Focus Pieces   32

Compliments   33

Plant Essences   34

Tiers and Dimension   34

CHAPTER 5   Selecting Crystals, Stones, and Metals   37

The Difference between Crystals, Stones, and Metals   37

Purchasing with Grid Making in Mind   38

Building a Gridding Collection with these Four Groups   38

Natural and Polished Shapes   39

Sphere   40

Cluster of Points   40

Pyramid   40

Double Terminated (including Vogels and some Pendulums)   41

Standing Points, Mountain Towers and Cones   41

   Cube   42

   Wand   42

   Cylinder   42

   Heart   42

   Blades and Fans   43

   Tumbled   43

   Chips and Beads   44

   Pendulums   44

Purchasing in Multiples of Odd and Even Numbers   44

CHAPTER 6   Selecting Layout Boards and Sacred Geometry   47

   Sacred Geometry and Common Symbols   49-55

CHAPTER 7   Cleansing Energy Fields   57

Crystals that Self-Cleanse   57

Singing Bowls and Tuning Forks   58

Vocal Toning from the Heart   59

Visualized White Light Envelopment from the Heart   59

Sage, Palo Santo Holy Wood, and Incense   59

Plant Essence and Oil Spray Mists   59

Moon Light   58

Sun Light 60

Cleaning your Stones, and Crystals of Debris 60

Special Note on Water and Salt Water 60

CHAPTER 8 Creating Your Crystal Alchemy Grids 63

Fields of Gratitude Guide 67

- Joy 71
- Safety 75
- Stability 79
- Well Being 83
- Creativity 87
- Success 91
- Freedom 95
- Romance 99
- Nurturing Love 103
- Community 107
- Purity 111
- Peace 115
- Spirituality 119

CHAPTER 9 Governing Colors Guide 123

Color Tones Matter 123

Shades of Red   123

Shades of Orange   127

Shades of Yellow   131

Shades of Green   133

Shades of Blue   135

Indigo, Purple and Violet   137

Aqua and Turquoise   139

Shades of Pink   141

Rainbows   143

White   145

Black   147

Clear   149

Earth Tones   151

Precious Metals   153-155

About the Author   157

Author's Note

Aloha beautiful crystalline beings! It is my privilege to share my art of crystal gridding alchemically with you. I am happy to say that it includes so much more. It's also about the interpersonal journey of spending thoughtful and heart-centered time with these magnificent beings of light, the crystal wisdom keepers. It's about developing a regular practice of cleansing the auric field and being in the state of gratitude, the highest vibration to be in resonance with. In this practice, we strengthen our alignment with the co-creative power and intelligence that dwells within us all. In so doing, we better realize our gifts of empowerment and graciously become more receptive to receive our Divine inheritance, according to the Divine will, through our living trust in this Omnipresence. We soon come to realize just how wealthy we truly are!

    This book is about realizing and utilizing a support system that we have always had at our service. As we practice holding our alignment with the Divine heart steady, the crystal wisdom keepers are there to hold the vibration steady, if we are ever pulled away from our heart center by fear. With practicing the methods shared in this guide, one's co-creative power and

Photo at left - " They tried to bury us. They didn't know that we were Seeds." - Dinos Christianopoulos

Ammonite, Clear Quartz, Amazonite, Rose Quartz, White Calcite, Lemurian Seed Crystal laser wand, seeds, seeding Bougainvillea flowers, Hibiscus flower buds, and a Pods music chime.

intuition will improve. The ultimate goal is to use our crystalline being as a walking 24/7 hologram projector, field stabilizer, amplifier, and as a living crystalline grid.

With regular practice, we remember how to walk in the flow of our co-creative power and mastery. It's about experiencing results that keep us encouraged to stay in our heart-centered gratitude, trusting in the abundance of the Divine will, allowing for it to flow through us and out into our lives. Fear creates states of energetic chaos, causing resistance that distorts the energy of appreciation, and cuts us off from our positive, co-creative power.

We cannot be in the state of gratitude and fear at the same time. So, to keep from being in fear, we practice being in gratitude, which is the purest form of love, the power that emits our light. If we fall into fear and shut down the flow, we will naturally feel confused, weak and vulnerable and will manifest that discord. It is with the power of love and gratitude that we create our dreams. It is with our inner light that we visualize our highest aspirations, creating holographic projections that can materialize with a steady flow of gratitude. My goal is to inspire others to reconnect with their natural co-creative abilities, through this gratitude practice, with these crystalline masters of light, the crystal wisdom keepers.

Creating crystal manifestation grids alchemically can become a deeply transformative experience when keeping present and reflective through the journey. From the uplifting clarity of energy purifying techniques practiced, to the use of gratitude based affirmations, making a mindful connection with the Creative Intelligence of all, and affirming for the goodwill of all to be made manifest, you are doing something profound in your life with this regular practice. Make sure to take moments to appreciate how special this art is for yourself, those you love and the world.

Photo at right - "Attuning with the Law of One" Aquamarine alchemy crystal singing bowl in the note of C# OM, the Universal/Earth Star chakra, Apophyllite tips, Clear Quartz pyramids and double terminated wands for program directing and power generation, Scolecite tumbleds for connection with the Divine, Aquamarine beads for eternal quality of Divine being, sea shells for their connection to the Universal consciousness, Silver beads and Petrified Wood for field stabilization, Swarovski crystals for rainbow brilliance, and a custom made (Law of One) activation/attuning wand.

Introduction

I graciously welcome you to this perspective on the wonderful practice of crystal grid making alchemically. It has been such a pleasure to create this guide, sharing my passion for crystal grid alchemy. My purpose is that others can find more value, meaning and use from their beautiful collection of crystals and stones with this practice. If you haven't started yet, it is time to put your crystals into Divine service!

I used to be in the business of assisting others with their purchases of crystals, crystal singing bowls, and complimentary products related to energy healing, holistic health, and meditation. I also developed deeply transformative crystal alchemical energy attuning treatments in my day spa, including a nurturing crystal smooth stone massage. We always had crystal alchemy grids, small and large, working for us on the retail floor and at crystal singing bowl gatherings on the beach and in the parks. Crystals played a role as important as oxygen it seemed. Even the water served in the day spa was *safely* infused with the frequency of crystals.

As customers noticed our grid displays, there were many common questions asked about crystals and crystal grid making from those new to crystals as well as those who had been working with them for decades. Realizing how many people were seeking to work with their crystals in a meaningful way is what truly inspired the writing of this book. After selling the business to honor the call to move back to Kauai, I wanted to continue sharing the wealth

Photo at left - "Lucidity Activation" Clear Quartz standing point center for program directing. Apophyllite tips for power generating and supporting lucidity, Charoite for supporting the waking dream state, Orange Calcite for joyful and empowered living, Pyrite for field stabilization, Clear Calcite for further grid support and amplification. Hand written Language of Light activation codes.

of knowledge that I had accumulated on the valuable ways to use crystals to enhance one's life, which I knew would be appreciated by so many if I shared it.

It is my goal that the information shared in this guide will answer most of your questions and even deliver beyond them. It is my goal from the heart, that by becoming familiar with this book and working with it, you will be creating crystal alchemy grids with great confidence and will be manifesting with great proficiency.

Though scientist like Marcel Vogel, who brought the use of crystal chip technology to the world of computers could explain how this works, he and his work remain relatively unknown. Regardless, many of us experience this special relationship with the crystals and their effects in our lives. I ask you, to trust with discernment, the conclusions that myself and so many others throughout history have come to about the metaphysical properties of crystals and their manifesting efficacy until you start to experience them for yourself.

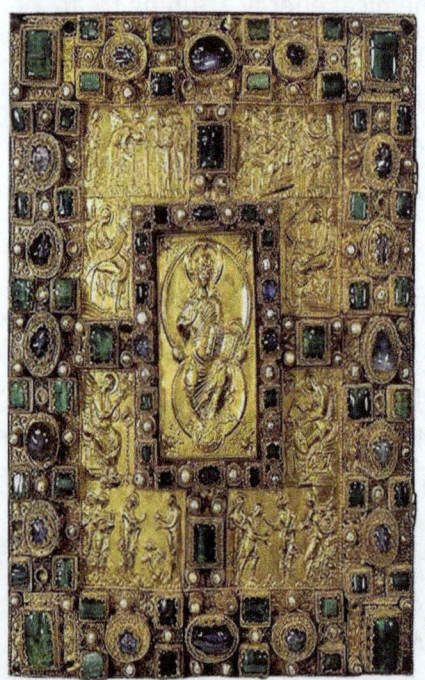

This guide does not intend to make any physical science claims and speaks completely to the metaphysical reality. Of course, this guide may also simply serve as a resource for creative and artistic inspiration. That alone is a beautiful gift. When we are inspired, we are In-Spirit!

Throughout history, it was the shamans, high priests/priestesses, seers, oracles, and royals who used precious gems in their arts, architecture, clothing, and medicines. It is no surprise to me that this was even more

Cover of the Codex Aureus. ca. 870 created for the Emperor Charles the Bald. The cover is of handmade gold, encrusted with precious gems of Sapphire, Emerald and Pearl. At the center appears Christ in Majesty. On his knee he holds a book inscribed with the words, "I am the way, the truth and the life. No man cometh to the Father but by me." I would call that an affirmation crystal alchemy grid. Stunning!

so during the times of our collective, deepest descent into the greatest of darkness and separation from the Radiant light behind all of creation. These points of light were one of the easiest ways to connect with pure, balanced and aligned energy during times of so much chaos, suffering, disease, and fear. How wonderful at such a time, to be able to close your eyes, hold a quartz crystal in your hand and feel the vibration of pristine, aligned life force energy, free from the distortions of human degradation, manipulation, and ego separation.

Moving forward in time, the connection to the crystal kingdoms kept their place in the lives of the wealthy, through their use of ornamentation and displays of grandeur. Thankfully, they have now found their way into a broader market space. Today, crystals are valued by everyday people: young and old, male and female, rich and poor. The timing is clearly ripe for this renewed interest in the metaphysical properties of crystals, where they play a new and valuable role now.

The modern world is facing new challenges dealing with distorted and chaotic patterns of light. With industrial and technological advances have come a new source of disturbance within our subtle energy fields and nervous systems, particularly experienced by those who are hyper-sensitive. The canaries in the coal mine, energy sensitives, and especially empaths, can be better supported by the stabilizing crystal and mineral kingdoms through resonance.

We are in a time of the gross misuse of synthetic chemicals, artificial frequencies and radiation coming from our commercial products, electronics and technology. As crystals, stones, and minerals are forming, they follow the original blueprints of creation, drafted by the crystal wisdom keepers of the telluric realm, receiving the pure light of creation. Unlike people, they hold the pure light stable. Their energy frequencies help to keep our field strong by the natural amplification of being in like resonance with us. Exposure to artificial chemicals and frequencies can shift our natural resonance out of that with the earth's resonance (Schumann wave) and we can become weakened. By attuning with crystals through appreciation, vitality may be enhanced as we resonate with them, akin to tuning forks.

Crystals themselves have their own reason for being, which is their love of the One that called their conscious light into service. This love generates a light so vast, pure, and brilliant that it is completely understandable why we feel drawn to pick them up and hold them. They feel good because they are a purer version of our crystalline being. We too are made up from the mineral kingdom and have crystalline structures within our bodies. Our DNA is so similar with crystals that only an expert could tell us apart under a microscope.

As we co-create within the fields of gratitude through the art of crystal grid making, we also fall into greater resonance with the crystalline aura of the new earth. Mother Gaia has all the light encoded programming in her blueprint required for planetary ascension. We are ascending with her when we actively come into resonance with her crystalline aura. Our light encoded filaments, within the blueprints of our DNA, become activated by these sparks of Divine light when we fall into resonance with her. This is why spending time in nature and appreciating its gifts, beauty and support for life are so important. This resonance triggers our light body to activate, open, expand and evolve, causing us to ascend with her.

It is important to me to include this scope of the greater value of crystals in our lives at these times. I hope to help inspire the natural crystalline alchemist within you. This book is encoded with frequencies and activation grids to do just that. And so it is. ~ from the heart

Derbyshire's all-quartz stone circle at Arbor Low in the White Peak District . Prehistoric crystal rock earth grid.

INTRODUCTION

"The new physics provides a modern version of ancient spirituality. In a universe made out of energy, everything is entangled; everything is one." Bruce Lipton

Medicine wheel at Medicine Mountain, Bighorn National Forest. The Indigenous Crow say that the Sacred Wheel was already existing, when they arrived, having been built by "ancient ancestors" or "people without iron." Used for prayer, vision quests, and receiving guidance. It is said to be astronomically complex. The wheel was made with Limestone which is composed in part of the minerals Calcite and Aragonite, both crystal forms of calcium carbonate. If it was used for prayer, it was in part used as crystal manifestation grid . An ancient crystal grid!

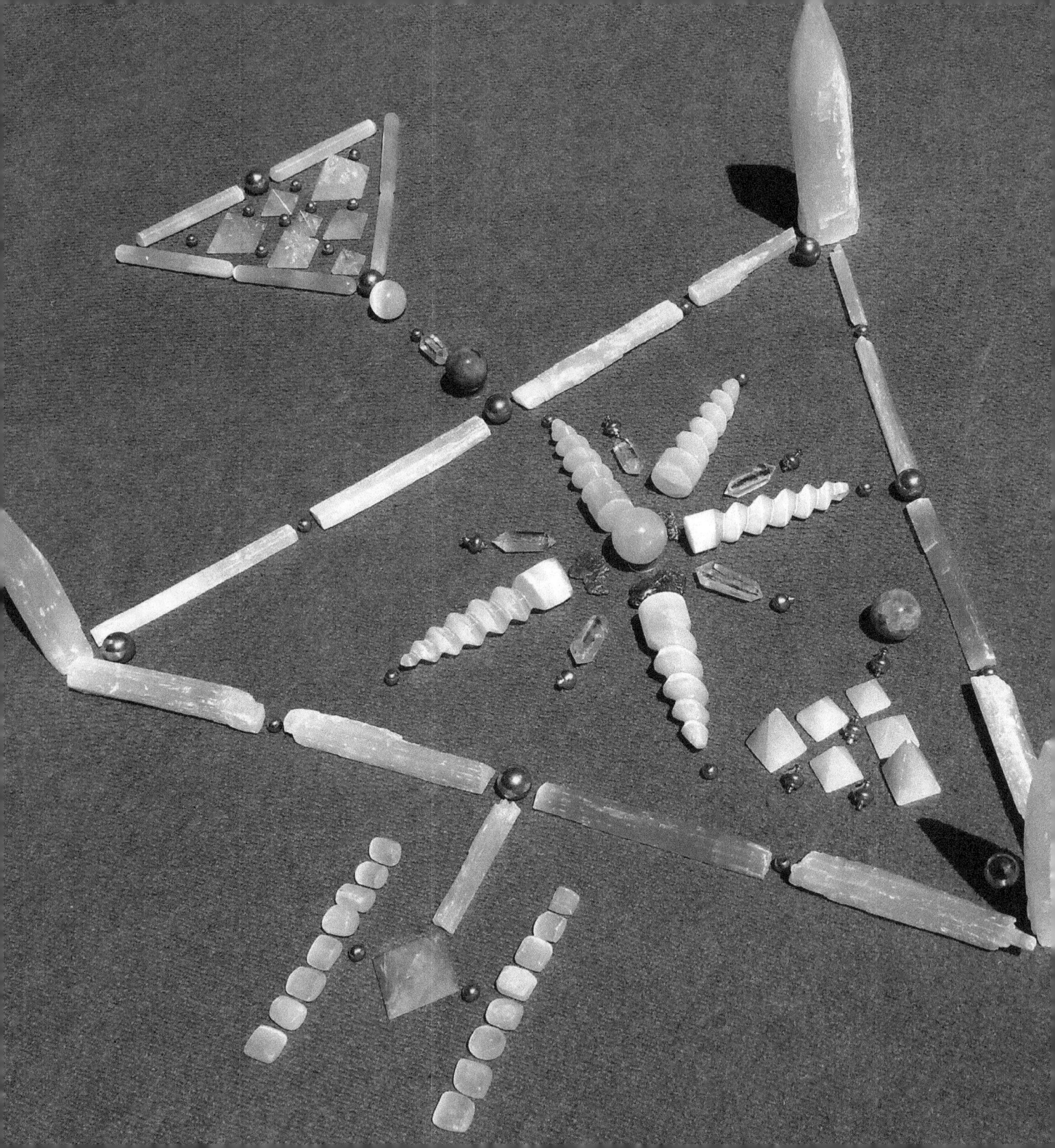

Chapter One

What is a Crystal Grid?

"The alchemy of good curating amounts to this: Sometimes placing one beautiful piece near another, makes one plus one equal three. Two beautiful pieces arranged alchemically, leave each in tact, transform both, and create a third." Jerry Saltz

A crystal grid is an organized grouping of crystals, and perhaps other items, which can include natural elements, sacred geometry, symbols, and more. Adding these other elements is where the alchemical art comes in to play. A manifestation grid uses the Universal principle of "energy flows where attention goes." Gratitude felt in the heart is one of the quickest and most powerful ways to pull in co-creative energy, so we use it when affirming to activate the crystalline field, once the layout is done. This activation creates a picture hologram in the grid field of what we visualize and affirm to be made manifest, working to attract its likeness into the material experience.

      Intuition tells many of us that the crystals are in direct alignment with the Divine and that they maintain the undistorted, original light of creation. Many people experience an intuitive relationship with the light of consciousness within the crystals. Their vibration is exceedingly high and it requires great clarity. This may explain why children are so adept at intuiting

Photo at left - This crystal alchemy grid was created for stabilizing the energy of a Triple Stargate Passage which included the solar eclipse of Sept 2017. Selenite, Labradorite, Copper, Citrine and Clear Quartz were used.

crystals. For these crystals to become manifesting grids, they must be activated. For many, it is like saying a prayer for blessings received. The fields of gratitude guide (page 67) provides a gratitude affirmation specific to each of the 13 fields we manifest under. They can be further personalized for your specificity.

The activation creates an energy field which holds the gratitude affirmation "active" in a field of potential. The laws of like-attracting-like through resonance go to work. Our crystal alchemy grids then act like a placeholder which helps to extend the time that we can be, "actively" in the manifestation process. We then place our trust into the higher laws of creation and miracles that govern our being and breath of life. It otherwise takes an adept multidimensional awareness to hold this field active until the results arrive.

These grids can also be created to generate and amplify ambient energy fields to live, work, sleep and play within. They can be customized to support meditation, communication within a family, study or creative pursuits. They receive, hold and transmit light information through the subtle energy fields at faster than light speeds. It can only take a moment to start shifting the ambient energy of a person, place or situation with a simple thought too.

Would you like to come home from a stressful appointment into an energy field of nurturing support and tranquility? You can. Just create a crystal alchemy grid in your home for it before you leave. The calming ambiance of tranquil energy will greet you when you arrive back home. As you walk in the door, tune into the blissful energy. That is my kind of smart house! Customers would walk into my retail store and spa and exclaim, "The energy feels so good in here." Some would start crying. Some would have headaches disappear. It truly works!

The greatest potency in the alchemical process comes from the heartfelt appreciation and the trust generated while arranging your pieces. When the heart energies, item selections, and layout design are working together; a unique energy field becomes generated. This field can be further purified from interference and amplified with the use of essential oils, aura clearing crystals like Selenite, and sound toning tools; your voice included. (page 57)

CHAPTER ONE

We can significantly amplify the field by affirming that all we aim to manifest, be made for the greatest good of all. This is where the miracles of the alchemical process begin to form. Once you walk away from your crystal alchemy grid, you can feel confident knowing that it is holding the gratitude affirmation active in the field of potential for you. They will weaken as they meet with resistance while at work. Crystal alchemy grids can be kept strong by coming back to them periodically to "freshen them up." We do this with a reaffirming of the gratitude affirmation and perhaps a misting of some essential oil, the lighting of some organic incense, or toning.

We are working with the Universal law of likes-attracting-likes. This means we need to create the field of attraction first. It is said, by those who can see into energy fields, that crystals can generate and hold a hologram image of the projection coming from the program activation. This is our field of attraction. This looks like when R2D2 projected the hologram message to Luke from Princess Leia in Star Wars. Science is currently programming 5-dimensional holograms into crystals with lasers. The physics of crystalline hologram programming is already in today's technology! Marcel Vogel suggests we can do this with thought alone.

A fun way to understand the power of likes-attracting-likes is to obtain two tuning forks tuned to the same hertz frequency. While holding them both, after you strike one and get it vibrating, the other will start vibrating all on its own, because of like-resonance.

Activating the energy is important. The tuning forks will remain silent until one of them is caused to become start moving in vibration. This movement in one triggers the movement in the other to join in. In the case of a crystal alchemy grid, it acts like the tuning fork that we first strike by activating it with the power of our gratitude, which acts as the striking force. The more powerful the striking force is, and the more often we keep the field humming by reactivating it, the greater we increase the power of the field of attraction.

Though we can use ourselves as crystals and our mental images as hologram projectors, it requires a very adept ability at maintaining 100% cognitive multidimensional awareness

to effect tangible results. With practice, it becomes easier to maintain such multidimensional focus. Practice using yourself as a crystalline energy generator on the go as well.

Sometimes our affirmations are left un-manifested. There can be many valid reasons for this if we feel certain that we have kept in the positive affirmation. The most probable reason for interference is that it may just be in too great of contrast with the soul life plans of yourself or any others involved. So, with grace and acceptance that there is so much more to our purposes for being that we may not fully understand, it's best to let it go for the greater good until another time.

All the codes of creation and sacred geometries are held within your DNA. The right energy and timing, along with the gratitude affirmations, act like keys that trigger the activation of these dormant codes to become active within us and allow for the flow of our greater being and potential to come through. The exercise of creating with the crystal alchemy grids helps us to experience and see this process in a tangible way so we can better act on it naturally. The crystals and grids become extensions of ourselves.

A calling to work with crystal alchemy grids is also about remembering how miracles are made through the practice of holding; goodwill, innocence, alignment, forgiveness, gratitude, and trust within a pure heart, even if we were to have nothing, but our breath to our name. It's about remembering how we play in creative fields of potential energy and using our imaginations as hologram projectors while resonating with our highest visions and dreams. It's about remembering to stay in the state of grace that is humble and worthy of receiving the gifts of life.

Photo at left - "Original Innocence White Flame 12-12 Portal Activation" Apophyllite tips, Clear Quartz pyramids and wands for program directing and power generation, Selenite tower at center, spheres, wands, tumbleds and spirals for purification, Amethyst wands, standing points and clusters, Amethyst Aura, Lepidolite tumbleds, Green Fluorite spheres and tumbleds, Angel Aura Quartz cluster, Scolecite tumbleds, Rose Quartz kites and tumbleds to support the field, and Blue Lotus flower essential oil diffusion with candle fire for purification and stabilization.

Chapter Two

The Living Power of a Crystal

"In a crystal we have clear evidence of the existence of a formative life principle, and though we cannot understand the life of a crystal, it is nonetheless a living being." Nikola Tesla

When evaluating the power of a crystal as a manifestation tool, it is up to us to experiment and take note of the effects and shifts that we experience when using them. This is not to say that renowned scientists have not made their discoveries about the living power of crystals. Nikola Tesla discovered and then spoke of crystals having a life-force energy of their own. He said for us to be mindful not to mistake them for inanimate objects. He further elaborated that they grow and can self-heal when damaged. He also found that they can record, store and transmit information. When Albert Einstein was asked how it felt to be the smartest man alive, he replied, "I do not know, you will have to ask Nikola Tesla." The smartest man according to Einstein told us that crystal are alive! Of course, if you are reading this, you probably already knew they were.

Like the electrical pulse that controls our heartbeat, crystals to have an electrical pulse. They have a heartbeat of their own. It is called the Piezoelectric effect. Crystals when under pressure do emit an electrical pulse that can be measured. Shungite has an electrical output so strong it can be measured with a simple voltmeter. This test can demonstrate that they are more than mere inanimate rocks to a layperson.

The human body is made of minerals and crystalline structures. The human body is an amazing biological accomplishment that exists and functions because of them. After all, our bodies become reduced to a pile of a crystalline mineral in the end.

Crystals are home to a consciousness that I refer to collectively as the crystal wisdom keepers. As part of the mineral kingdom, they have a connection to the telluric realm of the second dimension. This is where the blueprints for creation are drafted. All creation starts taking form in this plane. From the simple dot, the singular point of light of the first dimension, a line sprouts creating the second dimension. Sprouting within a polarized medium, like the negative and positive end of a magnet, the ends of the line are drawn to each other, creating the circle. Infinite lines sprout from particles of light creating more circles within the waveforms of electromagnetic energy. In this self-balancing act, the dimensions and seeds of life, take form.

Third-dimensional creation sprouts from out of the second dimension, the realm of the crystal and mineral kingdom. Because the crystal wisdom keepers are telluric beings, birthed from the pure and undistorted Light of creation, working with them brings us into greater alignment with our pure light being. We also begin to resonate better with our crystalline being and ability to draft blueprints of creation. Our physical bodies are fragile, prone to disease and decay. Our bodies are mortal. Pure Quartz has no half-life. It does not fall prey to radioactive decay. There is nothing more stable, pure, and true in an eternal expression of Divine light than the Quartz crystal. A Diamond will decay. A Quartz crystal is truly forever!

The second dimension is not inferior to the third. The third does not exist without it. Liken it to the sacral chakra. It is where the umbilical cord is connected. During a pregnancy, life force energy comes through it, causing new life to form. I acknowledge and honor the second dimension and telluric realm for keeping this plane of creation maintained and active for us. The telluric beings and crystal wisdom keepers are very present in this process.

A vacuum of air has no mass, smell, taste or feel yet its ability to cause a pulling force, makes its presence evident, as does the pulling force that draws us into the crystals we value. Think of the crystal wisdom keepers like telluric ambassadors of the Divine. That realm came before us, and we do not exist in the whole of creation without it.

There is no need to be a master at energy healing or technology to work in collaboration with these brilliant architects that are ready, able and willing to serve. Simply playing with crystals through creating interesting layout designs is a wonderful way to bring out the child within. A short meditation while holding them may even bring about a spontaneous healing or new insights. Gazing into the intricacy of their inclusions, fractures, and patterns can offer a much needed moment of deep and restorative centering too.

It's fun to play subtle energy sensing games while feeling their energy. With the eyes closed, see if you can tell two like-sized tumbled crystals apart from each other just by the way they feel. Keep them with you in a pocket for a day, gift them to others, decorate your home with them, wear them, nap with them, create crystal alchemy grids and experiment with where they find their place of joy, value, and meaning for you.

The beneficial effects that we commonly experience and share confirm their power to shift the energy in our worlds for the better. The more we share our experience with them and discover mutual ones, the more confident we can feel about their potential efficacy and value in our lives. The new discoveries we make and share can help to open up a new world of potential use with crystals and stones for others to explore.

Nikola Tesla spent years working with crystals and is quoted, "They are conscious living beings with awareness. They grow and have DNA just like us." The world of technology utilizes them for their ability to be programmed, record, and transmit information. It was Marcel Vogel, a research scientist for IBM, whose experiments into the living power of a crystal, lead to their use in computer technology. He later shifted to becoming a mystical scientist when he discovered that under specific conditions, plants could respond to thought.

"The crystal is a neutral object whose inner structure exhibits a state of perfection and balance. When it is cut to the proper form, and when the human mind enters into a relationship with its structured perfection, the crystal emits a vibration, which extends and amplifies the power of the user's mind." Marcel Vogel

He found that thought can be emitted in pulses which can create a coherent field with laser-like power. He found the most powerful and attracting field of coherence was that of pure unconditional love. He believed that it was within this medium that we discover the most important subtle aspects of life. He realized that this is why certain scientific investigations into the subtle realms cannot be replicated. It is because scientific protocols do not factor in the matter of relationships. This is why holding appreciation in your heart for what you are aiming for is so important. Marcel Vogel also said that what we tune into, we become attuned with. This is why it is important to be thinking about that which you wish to attract when selecting your crystals and creating your grids, with the love of your appreciation for the aim in your heart.

Crystals can hold frequency better than any other medium as of yet discovered next to our DNA, which makes them the excellent tools that they are, for holding our gratitude affirmations in play. Treat your crystals as if they are the conscious living beings with an awareness that Nikola Tesla found them to be, with love, appreciation, and respect and you will discover a new level of support in your life that asks nothing of you other than to keep them energetically clean. In your loving care and gratitude for them, they will be ready and waiting to be of Divine service to you in your next crystal alchemy grid.

Photo at right– Self healing Quartz Crystal point. When a quartz crystal is prematurely broken off from its matrix before fulfilling its growth potential, it will start to generate new points to heal the break and continue its growth.

Chapter Three

Common Questions

Can I create a grid to include more than just one affirmation?

Yes. Go for it! Reality beyond our five-sense perception is non-linear, quantum and multidimensional. Nothing is too much for the multi-verse to manage. However, for energy to come into manifest form, the way must be free and clear from any forms of resistance. Doubt, fear, anger, hate, sadness, hopelessness, frustration, impatience, and the such, lock the doors to our dreams. Just consider that the more dreams we are aiming to realize, the higher the probability is that interfering frequencies may be at play.

This is why clearing your auric field as the first step is so important. I do experience that regularly cleaning the grids auric field will make them the most effective. It's a good practice. If you are busy, incorporate crystals that also keep auric fields clean like Selenite, Shungite or Smoky Quartz. See page 58 for methods on cleansing the auric field of yourself and your crystal grids.

Special note—Crystal clusters that have lots of points are ideal for holding and directing multiple affirmation grids.

Photo at left - "Appreciating Mother Nature" Larimar, Rhodochrosite, Rose Quartz, and Petrified Wood tumbleds, Clear Quartz standing point, hanging pendulums and points, flowers and greens from the garden.

Do I need a layout board?

Any undisturbed space is ideal. You can use a spot on a counter or dresser top, coffee table, place in the yard, corner of a work desk, on the patio, or even the floor. Crystal grids can also serve as gorgeous centerpieces on a dining table.

If you use a layout board, it helps to treat it as a compliment to the grid. It is preferable to find something about a potential layout board that connects it either by color, material, symbolism, geometry or shape that will support the affirmation and helps generate a resonant field of attraction. Natural elements like wood and metals help to keep the fields stable too! This is not necessary. It's just an opportunity to add supportive energy or symbolism. See page 26 for ideas on layout boards you can find around the house.

Will my grids still work if I forget to cleanse the energy of my crystals between uses?

Not as well, unless in the least, you made affirmations to clear them while breaking down the previous grid where they were used. It's simple enough if need be. You can state a gratitude activation that they are cleansed and refreshed. Hold a mental image of them in a field of pristine white light and pour love and appreciation for their service into them from your heart. While selecting them for placement, simply affirm, "Giving thanks for your service, and with love in my heart, may all previously absorbed energies and programming be transmuted back to the pure light of their natural being."

Vocal toning with your voice is another simple way to ensure their purity. Toning the sound of "Ahhh" is the sound of the heart chakra and is easy for anyone to sing or hum aloud while they are selecting their crystals and stones. Keeping your crystals cleansed while the grid is in play is very helpful to your success. See page 58 for methods on cleansing the auric field of your crystals.

In this guide, I also suggest the use of what I refer to as the field stabilizers (page 28) that help with this. They are items that work to draw in and clear away any energies that may be creating a resistance block between ourselves and that which we would like to experience.

The fear-based energy of resistance is a like a sticky residue that, if built up enough in the fields of your crystals, will not allow your crystal to transmit the attracting frequencies, nor will they be able to receive new activation programming until cleared.

I must emphasize how much more effective and powerful your crystal alchemy grids will be the more they are cleansed and the more the gratitude statement is reaffirmed. Incorporating essential oil diffusers, sage, chimes, ting-shas, incense and singing bowls into your grids are nice reminders to regularly cleanse the energy of your grids and yourself.

How long do I have to keep the grid in place for?

As long as needed for you to be satisfied with the results. I have had some going for three months until results were achieved. I had also decided to give up early on some grids of lesser importance so I could use the crystals and stones for a new one. Many times the original motivation for the grid often seems not to matter anymore, which in itself, is a perfect result.

For some grids, I took them down before they became realized because I had a change of heart about it along the way and or the course of effects brought me to a new understanding that served as a valuable shift of energy just the same.

What are good crystals to start with?

Your favorites! When a crystal calls to you and grabs your attention, it is telling you that it wants to work with you. Those are the ones that most resonate with what is going on with you at the time and want to be at your service. These may change over time as well. For example, though Celestite generates one of the purest frequencies for peace, if a Labradorite keeps getting your attention, it will have a value in your peace grid, and I say use it. The crystals that call to us seem to sense where we are energetically depleted, out of balance or out of alignment, and they naturally work to set things right if we are open to their healing energies.

Pay attention to the crystals that keep drawing your attention to them. Use them in your grids along with those that have supportive properties. That aside, a Clear Quartz is the perfect crystal to start with and is truly the only one you need. For specific suggestions on purchasing with grid making in mind, please see page 37.

Are there crystals and stones that do not combine well together and how would I know?

If you just stuffed them in your pocket and ran, perhaps you will not experience them the way you would if you only had one in your pocket or two complimentary ones at a time. In my experience with crystal gridding, it is not as much of a concern. With crystal gridding, our activation program and the program directing crystal is what brings their frequencies into resonant alignment. Your program directing crystals (page 28) are like the conductor of a symphony orchestra. Your gratitude affirmation is the music sheet, and the crystals and stones are the musicians. When the stones and crystals play what is on the music sheet and follow the conductor, a Divine symphony is performed. Combining crystals with different properties is not of concern when practicing crystal gridding in this way.

Now, if you removed the conductor from the orchestra hall and left the musicians to play what comes most naturally to them, you *may* experience the feeling of jumbled noise. I myself act as a powerful attuning wand and so have not experienced this myself. I believe you can put a crystal alchemy grid in your pocket or a medicine pouch and go. Just include a quartz, a field stabilizing piece, and a gratitude affirmation. Because Herkimer Diamond brings cohesion to any field of chaos, you can always just include it and feel confident that your grid is playing a finely tuned symphony. Herkimer Diamond is a crystalline structure so it can also work as your program director and power generator.

I highly recommend creating an essence of Herkimer Diamond that you can lightly spray on them. Use a cobalt spray bottle, add a small Herkimer Diamond, some distilled water and a few drops of ionic silver or isopropyl alcohol as a preservative to keep it fresh. When feeling scattered or pulled in a thousand directions, you can mist it on yourself too! It feels amazing!

I would like to mention that, as with all things in life, there are complimentary contrasts. I included an additional fail-safe by adding the color palettes guide for each field of gratitude. The color pallets derived from the frequencies of the colors themselves, is not the same as the decorators color wheel, though you can refer to one if you are simply seeking complimentary balance with your grid. The color palette in this guide is drawn from the functions of the chakras that work together and support each other the best.

    I trust the chakra system because I have been working with it for almost three decades. For example, green supports the heart chakra which is our natural energetic balancing point. The combined gravity from the deep eternal wellspring of the heart chakra and the 40 times greater electromagnetic output than from that of the brain makes it a powerful force of bringing things to the center. Green is the governing color for this function. It will work to balance the properties of any other color crystal or stones you combine with it to quite a fair degree. Also, whereas a home decorator may cringe at the contrast of putting green right next to yellow, the two colors together in a grid can support a gratitude affirmation for generating an abundance of love or material wealth, perhaps even better than one of red and gold. Follow the color palettes guide reference in the fields of gratitude and you will be fine!

What is the difference between an alchemy grid and simply an artfully arranged collection of crystals and other materials?

    An artfully arranged collection of crystals is always pleasing to the eye, mind, body, and soul. But their full potential as a manifestation grid is not realized until they become activated with an affirmation program. The gratitude affirmation program ignites a hologram in the field of potential and keeps it charged for as long as the field stays cleansed of resistant energies. Imagine little helpers running about in the ethers looking for what is standing between you and that which you would like to manifest. As they find doubts and fears and feelings of unworthiness etc., their neutralizing power will work to clear the path. The more resistance that stands in the way, the more your crystals will need these cleansing helpers working overtime.

    I do encourage spending some time on the artistry if you have it. Not only does this give you some quality time in a creative state, which is very healing, your intuition also becomes further developed. One day when I was working on grids for hours, my intuition became so honed in, I was walking to the phone and reaching for it just as it started to ring. There is more to it than just coincidence. Artistic beauty increases the energy of appreciation that gets put into your crystals, and you will have a more powerful grid in play as a result.

Some persons new to crystal gridding often begin by making pretty designs, though exclaiming they have no idea what it means. Many persons like to just create pretty crystal grid displays. And yes, it is a fun and therapeutic art in and of itself! They become manifestation grids when activated with a program. Why not make a simple gratitude affirmation for peace in the world before walking away from it? You could also offer up its beauty as an act of gratitude for all of the blessings in your life. On a side note, you may be intuitively creating activation/awakening encoded crystalline fields of light and not know that you are. Had to mention that for my code keeping friends out there!

I think some of the most beautiful crystal grids in terms of feeling, are the ones that come from pure inspiration. When we are In-spired, we are in-spirit. Grids that are 100% intuitively inspired and created are examples of effortless alchemy in motion. Why not direct the beautiful energy to be put to a specific use too and activate it with a gratitude affirmation?

Regardless, I support running with flows of creative energy when inspired. They always pay off in some form or another. It is like listening to someone speaking in the Language of Light. We may not understand the sounds literally, yet they feel good to the soul, and everything seems to be made better by them.

I like to make crystal gardens. Are they crystal alchemy grids?

Crystal gardens are simply Divine and there is a reason to create them. They are a way of giving thanks to the beauty of nature. The more we give thanks for everything under the sun and beyond, the more powerful our co-creative abilities become. See below for an example.

CHAPTER THREE

How does this art put my crystals into Divine service?

When creating crystal alchemy grids, we are deliberately aligning ourselves with our co-creative power in accordance with Divine will. We do this through the use of affirmations in a state of gratitude. We do this by being open to receiving from the limitless abundance of the universe. We trust that we are generously provided for, through our Divine will, which is inherent to all. There is deliberate action made to be in alignment with the Universal laws of creation, set forth by the Creator itself. The Divine conscious being of all, fulfills itself through us, realizing it's glory, joy and creative intelligence, by our co-creation with it. When affirming to cause a shift in energy for the greatest good of all, we are bringing "goodwill" into the world. We are truly putting ourselves and crystals into Divine service when we are creating this way. ~ from the heart

Photo above- A Clear Quartz crystal garden used to appreciate the beauty of some pink roses.

Chapter Four

Elements of Creating Alchemically

Creating a crystal grid alchemically is all about incorporating complementary and supportive elements. The synergy blend is where the alchemy takes place. Webster's dictionary describes synergy as *"a mutually advantageous conjunction or compatibility of distinct elements, resources or effort."* These methods increase the dynamic for transmuting and shifting fields of potential. These methods work to provide a picture of the goal in the field of potential (a hologram projection that acts like a blueprint for creation) and a pathway free of resistance.

The word alchemy in this practice implies an art of *transformation* and *creation*. The minerals (crystals, stones, and metals) that we use in this art were being influenced by the forces of nature during their development. They are able to pass the signature influences of the air, water, fire, and earth on through their complex frequency output. We can add the fifth element of plasma, which like lightning, is represented by the striking force of the gratitude affirmation that activates the program for the crystal grid field!

A Gratitude Affirmation creates a Field of Gratitude

By affirming with gratitude that which we wish to manifest, we are soft programming the crystals with a co-creative directive. This is called activating the grid. In feeling and thinking about

Photo at left - "Heart Chakra Tune Up" Ruby in Fuchsite spheres and tumbleds, Amazonite tumbleds, Rose Quartz heart and raw Ruby chips. Heart chakra, note F, crystal singing bowl for the supporting layout board.

that which we wish to attract, we become attuned to it. As resonators of frequency, we can then attune the crystals that we are working with to our hearts vision. The crystals then generate this vibration, creating a field of attraction, a field of potential or what I like to call a field of gratitude. It acts as a placeholder to keep the energy of gratitude, love and the vision active. A heart full of gratitude can create miracles. Research has shown that the heart has an electromagnetic output forty times greater than that of the brain. Crystals speak the language of the heart and are in best in their Divine service with us when we are in our in our heart center. If you want to be a powerful co-creator, stay in your heart.

The featured fields of gratitude in Chapter 8 (page 67) all come with a general gratitude activation statement that can be customized for specificity. This is to be said at least once when the grid is complete. I begin saying it as I am selecting the crystals. It's my way of getting the field of potential warmed up. Repeating it as I am gathering items for the grid also helps me to begin gathering intuitive guidance on what other crystals, stones, compliments and designs that may be especially supportive for the specific goal of the grid. That is also how I came to gather much of the information suggested in this book after years of practicing the art this way and finding what has worked to bring the best results. Of course, you can choose to draw from the guide only. By opening to intuition as well, you may be lead to incorporate something personal that you have around the home that will make for a potent compliment. The guide is there for quick and easy reference to expedite one's proficiency. Our intuition will always be the best reference guide for navigating our personal path and endeavors.

When manifesting with gratitude in general, there are valuable insights to consider. We have been programmed to believe that most all of what we receive has to come about through hard work or a methodology. Our capacity to imagine how something can come to be is held captive by these restraints. If we are going to soar with the eagles, we have to set the process free to fly high!

The multi-dimensional aspect of our Divine being, and that of the crystal and mineral kingdoms, is always aware within the quantum field of limitless possibilities and potential.

Marcel Vogel was using crystal technology to take photographs of things remotely (out of sight) and even from the future. (See marcelvogel.org) One would postulate that the ability for that same crystalline intelligence to draft a coherent field of attraction, for that which is in our hearts, is truly out of this world. The creative intelligence inherent in all living things has a reach that is immeasurable. The more we put constraints on how and when something can be brought to fruition, the greater we may compromise the co-creative process with the crystal wisdom keepers and the Divine Architect, hindering our aim and the reach of our goal.

There have also been times where I was asked to take a second look at some things that were already well within my reach, and I simply was not recognizing and appreciating them enough for the realization to occur. Sometimes what may seem like a failed grid is simply a coconut to the head, asking us to look again and take notice or action or both.

Another important reason why an affirmation may not come to fruition is that the intended result would mean compromising the alignment of a soul path not in one or more persons highest and greatest good. This is the same thing as having an *intention* for your crystal grids. I use to use that word until I realized how much more powerful an *affirmation* was over an *intention*. Intentions put our hopes out in front of us, and they are weaker there because they are what we want *in the future*. An intention says, "I *want* for this to be made so." An affirmation says, "It *is* being made so now." As an intention, our aims remain outside of the power of the now. An affirmation is a commanding statement made in the now, which is where all of our co-creative power is.

Clean Energy

The cleansing of energy is very important. If there are stagnant or discordant energies in the field, they will create blocks of resistance which can compromise the function and flow of the grid leading to poor results. Do not skip these steps. See Chapter 7

Some energy cleansers such as Sage, essential oil mist, and a Tibetan singing bowl.

(page 56) for specific ways to cleanse the fields.

There are a few serious reasons for why this is important. Your crystals may be carrying some prior programming that you do not want running active in a new grid. Depending on where you received them from and how they were cared for by their last guardians, they may be polluted, especially if they were used to help with healing work and were not cleansed. They may literally have absorbed the energy patterns for some serious diseases. All new crystals that come into your life and home should be cleansed right away.

We also want to cleanse our auric fields of any fear-based resistance we may be carrying that has been keeping us in energetic dissonance from that which we wish to manifest. Negative energy is that which negates something and works to "take away" from a positive balance. Negative energy runs counter to creating a positive experience. This may be the ener-

gy of fear, doubt, anxiety, skepticism, discouragement, unworthiness, resentment, bitterness, anger, confusion, frustration, uncertainty or even conflict with others. This can also include beliefs about what can be, or how it can become, etc. Fear-based states also drain us of our vital life force energy making us weaker projectors of the holograms or can cause us to create very undesirable holograms if fear is running the imagination (images-in- action). This will all come about much easier if at first you play a crystal singing bowl, sing a song, mist some natural essential oil overhead, burn some sage, or meditate and then come into gratitude.

Cleansing is Charging

According to Marcel Vogel, though crystals are energetic as they vibrate and emit a frequency, they do not emit their own force. They are, however, powerful amplifiers of the ambient energy around them and within them. This is why they feel as if they have a separate power. The more powerful a crystal feels in your hand simply means it is a better amplifier of the ambient energy. If the field is a thick, discordant haze, they will amplify the stagnation, making them feel weak. They can also become weak at the task when they take on a lot of dense energy. Some may transmute the energy very quickly and others will over a longer period of time.

Make it a goal to become sensitive enough to feel your crystals. It is like when you are sharing a room with a person who is sad, hyper-anxious, exhausted, angry, or frustrated. If the cause is relieved, the person comes back into their natural balance, and they feel pleasant to be around again. A crystal holding similar absorbed energy will feel just like that.

Crystals do become drained when transmuting a lot of discordant energies and need the clearing to amplify better. This is how we charge them. Page 58 details methods for keeping the aura of your crystals, fields of gratitude and yourself free and clear!

Layout Board or Undisturbed Space

A crystal alchemy grid works best in an undisturbed space where it can be left to set and shift the energy fields. A crystal grid layout board is anything that acts as a stable foundation which

THE ART OF CRYSTAL GRID MAKING

Sample layout boards of a moss mat, tree trunk slice, and a Sacred geometry symbol; the Flower of Life, fire burned onto a wooden disc.

Pyrite metal, Angelite stone and Herkimer Diamond crystal.

would ideally be made from an organic material to support the field. There are products on the market specifically created for this purpose. There are suggestions for items around your home that you can also work with at the beginning of Chapter 6. (page 47)

Let your imagination run free for unusual items to create your grid upon, such as using a mirrored tile for greater amplification, a natural woven dinner placemat, a favorite sacred geometry print, a wall hanging laid flat or even a plate charger. Creative types will draw their own on sketch pads even. I tend to prefer layout boards and cloth that have a single color tone. If there is a busy print that also has a lot of color variety, your crystals or intuited design may get lost in it, diminishing the visual impact.

Ultimately consider a place for the layout board or surface to be where you will be able to easily appreciate its beauty every day, a place where you will be able to freshen up the activation often and be able to cleanse the field regularly.

Crystals, Stones, and Metals

Crystals, stones, and metals are the essential components of your grids, and truly nothing else is necessary to create a powerful and beautiful crystal alchemy grid. In a broad sense, related to their alchemical use in gridding, the crystal represents air, the stone represents water, the metal represents fire, and the layout board represents the earth. Crystals, stones, and metals all have their own unique vibration and properties that they have been imbued with by the nature of their creation. You will enjoy building a collection with a wide variety of pieces that feel like long lost friends to you.

CHAPTER FOUR

Frequency Field Stabilizers

Frequency field stabilizers fulfill many important roles within the alchemy of crystal gridding. The ultimate task of the frequency field stabilizers is to hold a coherent field that is in alignment with the field of gratitude being affirmed. The goal is to keep the energy field strong and free of resistance and distortions from interference. We want the heartfelt messages we send to the Universe to go out; clean and clear, crisp and sharp, and to come back into our reality with equally consistent results. These are pieces that absorb negative energy that can clog up the gears of creation or that act as a weight helping to create the pull of gravity for the field of attraction.

Example Frequency Field Stabilizers

When manifesting for a material item; such as a new car or vacation, a denser, earthy piece can add the weight of resonance with the physical/material plane. When your affirmation includes manifesting in the subtle realms, for example, improved higher sensory awareness, the protective energies of your field stabilizing piece will work to neutralize any disturbances while you are opening up. When affirming for positive growth change; such as for a promotion, the black field stabilizing pieces will help to mop up the excess; fears, insecurities, worries and anxieties, that may stand between you, and what your greater Divine worth can command.

I have also found that if any of your colored pieces have black inclusions like Rhodonite or Iolite in Prehnite, they come with their frequency field stabilizer built-in. A smoky Citrine would also be able to fulfill every role. It generates color to support the field of gratitude, has quartz to receive programming and the smoky quality for stabilizing, protecting and clearing. Crystals on their original rock matrix also have the field stabilizer built-in.

There are a handful of affordable and easy to find crystals, stones, and metals that are my favorite go-to pieces for powerful field stabilizers. They can be any metal, such as Hematite, Pyrite, Brass, Copper, Nickel, Pewter, Silver, Gold, Titanium, and Platinum. They can be any black stone such as Onyx, Black Tourmaline, Shungite, Arfvedsonite (often mistakenly called Astrophyllite) and Apache Tear. They can be any root chakra stone such as Agates or Jaspers in deep earth tones (page 151). They can be any stone or crystal known for neutralizing negative energy such as Golden Tiger Eye and any stone or crystal known for protection and shielding such as Lapis Lazuli or Black Kyanite Blade.

Using the essential oil essence of any tree will do the job too. You can create a crystal water infusion and mist your grid, diffuse the oil with a tea light candle oil warmer or burn an organic incense stick. The roots of a tree hold the earth stable, the branches reach out into the heavens, and the leaves absorb the cosmic light and spread it over the earth through its fruits, nuts, and seeds. Trees convert dangerous carbon monoxide into life-giving air to breath. Trees pull the elements of creation into one stable body of being that provides a home for many life forms and bear the fruits and the seeds of new creation. Their essence is a powerful alchemical tool indeed. Clay pieces, natural wood or fiber cloth layout boards lend a helping hand.

Some sample power generators; Clear Quartz and Amethyst standing points, Quartz cluster, Orgone generator, and a Copper sphere.

Power Generators and Program Directing Crystals

Power generators are pieces that amplify the energy of the grid field or contribute energy in the case of an orgone generator or precious or semi-precious metal. Program directors are crystalline pieces that can receive and transmit the activation program. Any piece that has a quartz crystalline structure in it can do the job of both. You need just one for the program directing. But u as many as you like for generating more power or amplification, or helping with a multi-focused affirmation. The program directors transmit the program out into the other pieces and out through them into the Universe. Power Generators make the transmission strong.

Crystals with clarity, lots of points, and strong third eye or heart chakra properties, pyramid shapes and crystal singing bowls work well for these roles. Playing a singing bowl that has been incorporated into a grid daily will help to keep the field clean and strong. Sometimes I use a clear quartz point for the program director and a lot of copper or pyrite to amplify as well as stabilize the energy.

Sacred Geometry

Sacred geometry is considered by many ancient cultures and modern persons to be a blueprint of creation. They recognized patterns in nature which they understood to be the building blocks of the Universe and everything within it. They noticed patterns and cycles of transformation and abilities to self-replicate in these natural designs. Considered to be the fundamental laws of creation, these patterns are held sacred because they originate from the Source of all creation.

Behind all matter is found the fabric of geometric energy which formats the constructs of the material world. Knowing this makes sacred geometry an obvious and useful tool to incorporate into your grids. Man-made symbols will only hold a power of value given to the symbols by those who believe in their power. Sacred geometry symbols (page 50) that are innate within the creation of the Universe are purely aligned with the origins of creation itself. This intelligence becomes the field.

Some sample program directors; Quartz and Amethyst standing points, crystal singing bowl, Tangerine Aura Quartz cluster, Selenite and Quartz pyramids and points.

Examples of Sacred geometry compliments; Seed of Life, Golden Ratio and the Vesica Piscis.

Flower of Life

Grid Templates and Free Form Designs

Technically speaking, a grid is a network of intersecting straight lines. We see them used on paper or in computer programs used for plotting and designing. In these applications, they help to keep balance and scale. They can be used to route things in motion such as the power grids that run electricity out from power stations. We use them to control the flow of things such as traffic on our roadways throughout the land. Nature's grids are its river ways, and the nervous system pathways of biological life forms.

For our purposes, grids help us to organize our crystals into a coherent and balanced design. For our purposes, balance doesn't have to mean symmetrical. In gridding, balance is more a value of weight and color distribution. It's about how the pieces complement each other and the relationship of the energy that is flowing between them. Flow and synergy between the pieces is what you want to tweak and perfect with the design itself. If it doesn't *feel* right, take it away or move it around.

We are really creating with these crystalline grids, *fields of light* and *fields of potential*. These truly are brilliant fields of light that span the multiverse. In this book, you will not find any rules on laying grid patterns themselves. I am writing from my experience working with the crystal wisdom keepers and my own intuitive memories of working with the crystals in other lifetimes. Extrasensory memory of working with crystal energy in other lifetimes is what draws most all of us to work with crystals in the here and now again.

Gridding with strict rules had its purpose when humanity was deep in the darkness of the low end of the third density after the fall. Now that we are working in the age of light, we do not require the precise structuring of grid patterns to hold, move and emit light energy. This shift is akin to how we no longer need our corded phones wired to the wall, connecting wires with wires across the lands and seas to the next corded phone, wired to the receiver's

CHAPTER FOUR

wall. Just as we can now communicate with persons in space and on the other side of the world wirelessly, we are awesomely "wireless" once again with our crystal gridding. This long-awaited shift supports the efficacy of remote crystal healing too.

To illustrate with the wireless telecommunication analogy, the crystals, as always, act as their own receivers and transmitters, like the phones. The frequency field stabilizers and amplifiers now function as the cell towers and our hearts purity function as the satellites.

The telecommunications move through the field of space and in this light, it is more accurate once again to use the term "field" over the term "grid". Maybe it will catch on one day. We are really creating crystal alchemy fields of light. So, be easy on yourself when it comes to placement. Your gratitude from the heart, affirmation for the good of all and keeping in alignment with the Divine through trust is the crux of achieving results. When in doubt of your placement, Herkimer Diamond brings coherency to any energy field. Just add a piece and thank it for pulling your pieces together in support of your gratitude affirmation.

If your intuition is good, it is a great asset to creating the most potent grids in my opinion. Intuition has access to a higher awareness. It knows and sees beyond the limitations of the ego mind. Our greatest personal guidance comes from intuition. Playing with random layouts and pausing to feel them along the way and adjusting them to see how they feel differently is a great way in itself to develop your intuitive feeling abilities. The more clear quartz pieces that you work with, the faster your intuition develops, in my experience. Intuit = In-to-it.

As you step back and *feel* the crystals, one of the stones may be screeching at you. If so, remove it. Perhaps, the bottom half feels too heavy. Remove a few pieces or work a few of them higher up into your design. Maybe it gives you a tight feeling. Open up some hard lines and create more of a spray design in the corners and see how that feels. Feel and play, feel and play. Does it feel too hard-hitting? Add soft pieces like flowers or leaves or switch out some vibrant colors for pastels. Does it feel like the pieces are not relating? Connect them with many of the same things such as small quartz points, seeds, coffee beans or pour thin lines of sea salt or sand to make visual connections. When in doubt, start removing items by same groupings of like items or one of too many colors.

Working with free-form design evokes the power of the abstract. It is known that abstract art generates a greater emotional response from people. Emotion is energy-in-motion. A crystal alchemy grid is all about putting energy into motion to shift energy fields, which will materialize new potentials. Experimenting with non-traditional, free-form designs, inspired by abstract geometry is liberating and timely! Play with using curved lines, free-form and abstract designs and shapes that have symbolic and intuitive value to you. These all carry an added charge. Abstract grids put the dynamite into the dynamism they seem to pop with.

Focus Pieces

Example focus pieces.

Focus pieces would be something that can draw attention to the subject of the grid. For attracting material abundance, items tied to the goal such as pictures of a vacation destination, coins, treasure chests, etc., can be considered focus pieces. I even make grids to cleanse and re-program a special attuning wand that I have. The wand is the focus piece, the item I am manifesting a shift of energy for. Sometimes, it may be a glass of water that I want to charge for causing a shift in my being when I drink it. You can incorporate the symbol for something you want to manifest and anything you wish to bring about a positive shift in energy for.

You can use a picture of something specific you want to manifest such as a photo of people during happier times, or a photo of yourself when you were in better health. It can also be an actual item that you would like to shift the energy of such as; a bottle of vitamins, a used piece of jewelry, something you cherish that picked up the energy of a traumatic event, like being recovered from a disaster, etc. Although focus pieces are not necessary, they will enhance the clarity of the field for improved result potential.

CHAPTER FOUR

Complements

Complements can bring in symbolic and energetic support from many sources including the plant and animal kingdoms, the ocean, spiritual and sacred symbols, statues of Saints or ascended masters. You can use flowers, prayer cards, essential oils, incense, feathers, candles, seashells, pine cones etc. With spiritual symbols and angelic beings or Saints, it is best to use those that have a personal meaning and value to you. Your value in them is what gives their symbolism significant weight, added to the value others have invested in them. Powerful symbols help to make very effective additional supports to your crystal alchemy grids.

Using complements is also an easy and affordable way to create the look of an elaborate crystal alchemy grid when you do not have many crystals, stones, or minerals to work with and really want to create a work of art to appreciate. Using a dozen of the same sized; seashells, pine cones, flowers, leaves, feathers, freshwater pearls, seeds, sea glass, coffee beans, slices of fruit, acorns, or coins, can make a powerful visual impact while adding symbolic energy to the field of attraction.

Example compliments.

For example, if you are creating a "new beginnings" crystal alchemy grid, it would make perfect sense to use seeds. For symbolic support with a Caribbean beach getaway, you could incorporate a collection of sea glass, sea shells and or create the alchemy grid on a plate of beach sand. If it is for material abundance, incorporate a valuable collector's item you have or a piece of valuable jewelry or photos of what you associate with material abundance. It's about incorporating the energy imprint into the field of what they symbolize and mean to you.

Essential Oil Diffuser and Spray

Plant Essences

Essential oils are supportive compliments to any crystal alchemy grid. They can be used through diffusers, incense, sage, and spray mists. Used in a tea light candle oil warmer diffuser, they can lend the support of the element of fire which is also noted to enhance many of the gratitude affirmations involving a need for action, ambition, transformation or warmth. Many essential oils also hold the creative blueprints for that which you wish to bring into your experience, such as a calming effect which Chamomile oil can support or an energizing effect with some spice oils like Ginger or Cinnamon. If you want better grounding, (I use the word stabilizing for a profound reason and suggest doing the same) use a sturdy tree oil like Cedar Atlas.

Tiers and Dimensions

Tiers are layout platforms that give dimension and height to the overall design. Tiered dessert serving trays work well for this or even a shelving unit. All sorts of items can create the pillars if you want to stack plates or boards such as large cylinders, bottles, bookends, or drinking glasses. Crystal wine glasses make gorgeous columns for stacking plates to create tiers with.

Where tiers provide multi-leveled grids, you can also create multi-levels upon the same single layout board or platform. This is an easier way to give your crystal alchemy grids some simple dimension for added interest, depth and movement of energy. Many gridders add dimension by stacking smaller pieces on top of larger ones, or by placing pieces on display risers.

Photo on right - "Spiritual Alignment" Amethyst standing points as power generators and program directors, Amethyst tumbleds to support the field of gratitude, Selenite spheres, mini towers and tumbleds for purity.

CHAPTER FOUR

Chapter Five

Selecting Crystals, Stones, and Metals

The Difference Between Crystals, Stones, Minerals, and Metals

All crystals, stones, and metals are minerals. Crystals are a unique class of mineral. They are formed from liquids that have crystallized into a solid structure of repeating patterns. It is this repeating pattern that makes a mineral a crystal. Some crystals have easy to see patterns, such as Fluorite, or Chevron Amethyst. Other crystals have very tiny crystal structures that to the eye make them look like stones; but they are crystals, such as Aventurine. They must also be inorganic, and not made from an organic plant such as a sugar crystal.

Stones are another class made from non-metallic mineral matter. Stones are compounds of various minerals that look smooth and opaque in appearance. All stones are minerals. Metals are also in the mineral family; however, their hardness and shine put them into a unique class of minerals called metal elements. Since they all belong to the mineral family, we are working with subgroups I will refer to as crystals, stones, and metals. Please note that I do not claim to be a mineralogist. The subtle energy fields are my specialty!

Photo at left - "Divine Empowerment Activation" Clear Quartz crystal standing point, Scolecite wands and tumbleds, Apophyllite tips and Snow Quartz tumbleds. Pyrite tumbleds and pendulum points.

Purchasing with Grid Making in Mind

There are some helpful tips I can offer when building out your gridding supply list and collection. Start with collecting crystals and stones that call out to you. We have a stronger intuitive connection to that which we are in most resonance with. Just being with resonant crystals and stones that you have an appreciation for is the beginning of the magic to come. Through the power of the appreciation our love for them puts us in, we naturally become more of an attractive magnet for other things that we appreciate in life.

Building a Gridding Collection with these Four Groups

Frequency Field Stabilizers - Black and earth tone stones, Clear Quartz and metals. (page 27)

Program Directors/Power Generators - Clear Quartz or any crystalline structure, double terminations and standing points, clusters and spheres. (pages 28 and 29)

Colors of the Rainbow – Primary colors, followed by the secondary colors and then the pastels. These will be what support the frequencies in resonance with the field of gratitude that you are working with. For example, using greens for healing, and blues for peace and calm.

Cleansing Supplies - Essential oils, diffusers and oil warmers, sage, organic incense, singing bowls, or chimes. There are plenty of interesting tools for keeping the auric field of yourself, your grids and your sacred spaces clean and aligned. (page 58)

When looking for pieces to act as program directors, power generators, and frequency field stabilizers, some pieces can play triple duty and are great if you are on a tight budget. A simple quartz crystal on a Pyrite matrix can act as a power generator, frequency field stabilizer, and programming director all in one.

High vibration crystals will accelerate the energy of the field and speed things up. Black Tibetan Quartz is a high vibration crystal that is relatively affordable, relatively easy to find and plays all roles. It is said that the Tibetan monks who gather it from the mountains, feel and hear it vibrating with the sound of Om. "Auuuuuuuuhm"

CHAPTER FIVE

Collecting a wide variety of colors is where the larger investment and build-out occurs, especially if you purchase them in groupings of multiple pieces. Each color, starting with the most powerful of the primaries, governs different planes that we can shift energy within such as the physical-red, mental-yellow, emotional-blue and spiritual-clear. By having crystals, stones, and minerals that represent the primary and secondary colors we can affect shifts in any of these planes more easily through resonant amplification.

All newly acquired crystals, stones, and metals should be cleansed of the energy of the previous owner or store they came from and always before creating a new grid with them. Please see page 58 for methods on cleansing.

Natural and Polished Shapes

Crystals, stones, and metals can be found in a variety of natural and polished shapes. Shapes can certainly lend the energetic properties of their geometry to the affirmation and thereby influence the energy flow of the grid. For example, pyramids are great for raising and focusing energy. Spheres are great for a soft diffusion of energy. Because they can have such a powerful influence in a variety of uses, I find them to be very valuable in an alchemy grid making collection. Here is an easy guide for the most common ones you will find and probably already have a few of.

Sphere

Spheres are ideal for shifting the energy of spaces without it feeling overwhelming. Spheres diffuse energy out softly into a space, as opposed to the concentrated flow directed by a crystal point. For example, a sphere power generator would be ideal for a grid created to enhance a safe feeling in a space for a new pet in the house, or for a small child or elderly person's room. They make great power generators for a "well rounded" reach and program directors to the other pieces within the grid for this reason. Spheres also symbolize unity, oneness, the

Selenite sphere.

whole, what is without end. A Selenite or clear quartz sphere is a highly valued workhorse.

Cluster of Points

Amethyst cylinder cluster, Angel Aura Quartz cluster and a Spirit Quartz cluster.

Clusters are ideal for affirmations that are multi-focused, where you need them to be far-reaching or to affect many persons, places, and things. An example would be affirming for many things to come out of one grid such as; bonding between multiple family members, cooperation at the workplace amongst coworkers, multiple health issues being resolved, peace amongst warring nations and perhaps success with a series of upcoming tests. The clusters, with their many points, can better direct the energy of a multi-focused grid. They make great power generators and program directors for this reason.

Pyramid - *Platonic solid associated with the element of Fire*

Amethyst pyramid.

Pyramids support affirmations that require a person or people to take action. They are also supportive when working with any third chakra issues such as building confidence and motivation or soothing aggression. They are also very supportive in grids where specific lofty goals aim to be reached. They are used in Feng Shui for wealth and career building. In general, pyramid shapes work to focus and raise energy as well as amplify the energy field of a grid.

Double Terminated (including Vogels and some pendulums)

Double terminated crystals and stones are shapes that have a focused point on both of the long ends of the piece. This feature can be found either man-made, such as with a Vogel cut crystal or natural, such as with a Herkimer Diamond. It is taught that double terminated crystals can both transmit and receive energy. Yes, they can. Any crystal or stone with quartz inclusions or crystalline structures can receive your programming and send it out into the field of potential, even if it is a tumbled. Quartz computer chips and wafers both receive, store and transmit programming and they are not double terminated shapes. They are flat squares and flat discs.

I like how double terminations can create a visual connection that unifies the pieces when a wide variety of crystals and stones are being used or when I want to demonstrate a specific flow of energy between pieces. I usually place them between the largest ones and or the ones that are the most different. These "connectors", placed between your program director and a focal point, can help to keep your program focused amidst a sea of supporting pieces. They encourage communication between specially selected stones and crystals.

Quartz Crystals with double terminated points.

One Herkimer Diamond can do this for the field as well. It is excellent at bringing cohesion to random and chaotic energy fields. I highly recommend having at least one, even if it were a tiny piece and used in a bottle for making a water diffusion spray.

Standing Points, Mountain Towers, and Cones

These all work to attract and amplify Universal energy. They make great power generators and program directors for this reason. They can also make very powerful frequency field stabilizers when you direct them to accumulate pure creative energy. If you have them, use them often, as they are awesome at these tasks. One tall standing crystal point is ideal to have in a collection. Clear quartz is preferable, though any piece with a crystalline structure will do the job such as Amethyst or Rose Quartz.

Selenite mountain, Amethyst and Quartz standing points.

THE ART OF CRYSTAL GRID MAKING

Selenite cube.

Cube - *Platonic solid associated with the element of Earth*

Cubes are ideal for grids that are working with root chakra issues such as health, finances, stability, and security. Cubes are also perfect for grids with "castle in the sky" goals, that will require strong foundations to build upon. They also play the symbolic role of a fortress, making them supportive pieces in protection grids. The cube structure can also symbolize something "established", making it a great compliment for manifesting what you want to last for a long time.

Wands

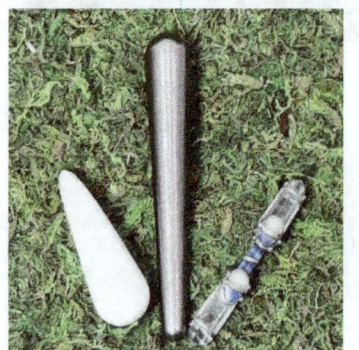

Scolecite, Titanium, and Quartz wands.

Traditionally, wands in a crystal alchemy grid would be used to program the grid for activation and drawing connections between the pieces for cohesion, but I believe this is no longer necessary. I feel that when we connect to the grid pieces with our heart, while saying our gratitude affirmation, the energy of love acts as the most effective force of cohesion. I like to use wands to symbolize the direction of larger flows of energy with the wider end being the receiving and the slimmer end being the transmitting. You can also create the outlining of shapes with them.

Cylinder

Shungite cylinders.

The energy of a cylinder generates outwards from the sides. They make good connectors at intersecting points for this reason. Selenite and Shungite cylinders are very effective at keeping the field "clean" and free of resistance. Cylinders are also ideal to use as support columns for holding up tiers in a multilayered grid and can also be used in place of an infinity symbol. In projective geometry, a cylinder is simply a cone whose apex lies on the plane at infinity.

Heart

Hearts are powerful symbols for the energy of love, from romantic to nurturing and even Universal. Of course, they are perfect for any grid dealing with a broken heart or betrayal wounds, as they will bring focus to the area in need of healing energy. Hearts also bring warmth, joy, the energy of optimism and sound well being.

Rhodochrosite heart.

Blades and Fans

The natural shape of a blade or fan; such as in Wavelite or Kyanite, makes them ideal for radiating energy. Black Kyanite Blade is the best of the best for sealing and mending holes and tears in the auric field. This stone enhances the power of a person or field of energy, exceptionally well, because it repairs any leaking drains. I recommend obtaining at least one Black Kyanite blade for your collection.

Black and Blue Kyanite blades.

Tumbled

You can find almost all crystals in a tumbled form, and they make obtaining the energy of rare and precious gem crystals more affordable, such as with Ruby or Emerald. Consider collecting your favorites in a grouping of three to six pieces. Using several or more of the same element or color in a grid helps to bring balance and cohesion to it.

Visually speaking, tumbles create softer appearing grids with the uniformity of their size and soft curves. Raw and rough pieces do generate a powerful energy field of potential and add interest. I tend to obtain mostly tumbled pieces for gridding as they do double duty for me. They travel well in pockets and are more comfortable for throwing into the bed at night. In some cases, as with Malachite, the tumbling and polishing process makes them safer to handle too.

Selenite, Scolecite and Stilbite tumbleds.

Apophyllite tip center piece, Larimar, Orange Calcite, and Azurite-Malachite beads.

Pendulums and quartz points.

Chips and Beads

Authentic chip and bead bracelets and necklaces are an excellent source for adding a lot of new crystals into your grid making collection. These smaller pieces contribute to the vibration and add accentuating detail that brings a sense of depth and dimension. Just cut the strings, and you'll instantly have dozens of mini crystals and stones to grid with.

Pendulums and Points

Consider collecting some of the same stones or crystals in pendulum or point form. Many crystal shops carry a few that are simple and more affordable to purchase in small quantity. Remove the chain and then use them to create points of radiating energy, or to show movement.

Purchasing in Multiples of Odd and Even Numbers

Purchasing the same stone or crystal in a quantity of three or more will dramatically change the way your crystal alchemy grids look and perform. With at least three, you can create the three corner points of a pyramid base to work around. With four of the same, you can create a square or a diamond shape by placing one in each corner. With five, you can create a star as your base, and with six you can create a circle or tetrahedron base to work around.

Several pieces of the same color can help to create a feeling of balance and cohesion. Having three or more of the same crystal or stone also lends more emphasis to the energy of that crystal or stone. Use groups of the same thing in even numbers when you are looking to calm, slow down and better stabilize chaotic energy fields. Use groupings of odd numbers when you want to stimulate new growth, change and open up new space.

CHAPTER FIVE

When building your collection, gather items in groups of three, four, five and six.
I wanted to show a sample grouping of groups and give some examples of the different
layout designs that can be created with them. I wanted to set them next to the look of
grids created with a random variety of single pieces. You can also feel
the difference bewteen creating with evens, odds or by mixing.

Sample groupings of threes, fours, fives, and sixes.

Created with a variety of single unique pieces.

Odd Numbered
Groups are
Energizing

Even Numbered
Groups are
Calming

Mixing Odd and Even Groups adds
Dimension and Interest

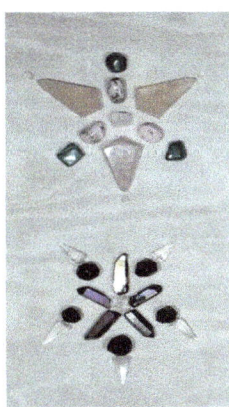

Top is created with
groups of three and
the bottom is created
with groups of five.

Top is created with
groups of four and
the bottom is created
with group of six.

When mixing Odd and Evens, the predominant
group is what will set the more energzing or
calming vibration. If they are equally used,
they will simple balance out to feeling pleasing.

"Light Body Calibration Attunement" Clear Quartz standing points, clusters, pyramids and double terminated points, Fluorite tumbleds and octahedrons, Apophyllite tips, Amethyst Aura tumbleds, Rose Quartz Tangerine Aura tumbleds and cluster, Angel Aura cluster, Spirit Quartz, and Celestite. Blanket Layout board from Café Press.

Chapter Six

Selecting Layout Boards and Sacred Geometry

Any clear surface, in an undisturbed space, can become the canvas for a crystal alchemy grid. A blank canvas can be intimidating to people new at crystal gridding who may prefer some guiding lines to follow for placement ideas. There are commercial Layout boards that come with designs to work your placements on. You can also use items with designs to for easier placement ideas such as; a Mandala print on a tapestry, or the power of a sacred symbol or geometry on a piece of framed art.

Layout boards can be something in a supportive color frequency or offer a connection to earth energy such as using a piece of wood or slate. Layout boards such as serving trays can even make your grid mobile around the home or office if needed. This works well for setting a field to sleep in. Just remove the tray from the bed when it is time to slip under the covers.

Spend the next few days looking around the house at what can be incorporated into your next inspiration. Here are some ideas.

*Table placemats   *Spare floor tiles   *Serving trays and platters   *Mirrors   *Cutting boards
*Cork boards   *Picture frames   *Decorative fabrics   *Blankets   *Books   *Candle Holders
*Bowls of water   *Tabletops   *Tree stumps outside

*Sand or salt layer- grid designs can be etched in before crystal placement.

CHAPTER SIX

Sacred Geometry

Sacred geometry refers to universal patterns of growth design, found in everything under natural creation. A design or pattern being universal and natural to all living forms means that it espouses Divine intelligence in its creation. This is what gives sacred geometry its sacred reference. Art, music, and architecture that follow the design patterns of the natural universe are considered sacred as well. The origins tie together geometry, mathematic ratios, harmonics, proportions, light, and cosmology. Sacred geometry is neither religious or "woo woo". It is supported by the scientific measurement of universal mathematics and principles of creation. By using sacred geometry and symbols in our layout designs, we incorporate the alchemy of being in alignment with the natural flow of creative energy and universal intelligence.

There are some common and basic designs that are truly fundamental for manifesting and they are recommended in this book. You can work with sacred geometry in a pre-drawn layout board or create the shape with the layout placement of the crystals themselves on a blank surface. The intersecting points of a grid are where energy concentrates. This is where

Photo at left - Fire burned "Seed of Life", sacred geometry layout board. Photo above is the natural unfolding of the Golden Ratio, or Fibonacci sequence found in everything.

we want to place our best power generators such as quartz points to maximize the potential.

Golden Ratio, Fibonacci Sequence, Phi

This symbol is considered the basic mathematical formula for all of creation. The golden ratio is what keeps proportion to scale as fractals repeat. It is found everywhere, from the placement of the knuckles on your hand; to the sunflower in your garden and the songs of the birds who sing in 432 hertz. I think this is the ultimate because of its brilliance to symbolically replicate our visual holograms to life-sized scale. Pine cones and sunflowers are compliments that offer a visual impact as well.

Vesica Piscis

The Vesica Piscis is created with two intersecting circles. It is symbolic of the Divine Feminine, merging of opposites, and point of creation. The Vesica Pisces is also symbolic of proportions in harmony. More potent to the alchemy of crystal grid making is that one circle represents the manifest world and the other, the field of limitless potential. The center overlap is the bridge where creation passes through and into the material world. These circles are the perfect place to put your supporting compliments with a focus piece in the center overlap.

Seed or Flower of Life

The Seed of Life represents the seven stages of creation. It is created with seven overlapping circles with the same diameter. The Seed of Life is symbolic of the blueprint for all creation and fertility. Its use can be found in all major religions and most ancient cultures.

CHAPTER SIX

Common Symbols for Crystal Alchemy Grids

"I don't deal in terminology. I deal with expressions: shapes, colors, tones, and characteristics." Savion Glover

Circle

The shape of a circle has many symbolic meanings: wholeness, completion, the self, the Infinite self, all-inclusiveness, simplicity, womb of creation, something without end, cycles, centering, and the celestial: sun, moon, and earth.

I think the circle and sphere always have a beneficial place in any crystal alchemy grid because they are found at the origin of all creation. I also like to incorporate the shape into a design where I want a soft and gentle effect into the field.

Take note that circles are also symbolic of the energy that is without end. If you want to bring swift resolution to a situation, use short pyramids or be very specific that you intend to use the circle's alchemical energy for completing a cycle or pattern. If you want to break free from something, or be open to new opportunities, create a circle with an opening.

Oval

Ovals provide all of the symbolic energy of a circle and yet are unique if you want the focus to be on the nurturing, feminine principle. This is not to be confused with the female sex. Males have nurturing energy. Associated with eggs, they bring the energy of new life potential. This is a good shape symbol for the start of new projects; new chapters in life; new beginnings and any new creation you wish to manifest.

Triangle

Triangles represent dynamic tension causing active motion towards a focal point. They are ideal for bringing in the energy of building upwards towards a pointed goal from upon a stable foundation. This makes it a popular shape to work with when you want to build with a goal in mind, such as pristine health, wealth and success.

The very assertive energy force of the triangle makes it aligned with the masculine principle. This is not to be confused with the male sex. Females have assertive energy as well.

Squares and Rectangles

These are often the most common forms people use when creating or building something because they offer a feeling of balance and conformity. These shapes for many provide a natural sense of trust and stability. They are symbols of security, safety, and strong foundations. Their alchemy is powerful when used to support other shapes created *inside* of them.

Cross

A crossing of two lines at the horizontal and vertical axis **+,** represents spirituality, religion, balance, unity, faith, hope, connection and the tempering of two forces. This can also be symbolic of the four directions of wind, air, earth, and sky. When formed with crossing lines at the diagonal like an **x,** they can add more stability to the energy field of the grid. Either are supportive when you want to unite and connect people, places, things and even conflicting emotions or thoughts.

Infinity

This symbol traditionally looks like a figure 8 on its side. There are several versions of it. Use the infinity symbol for affirmations that are meant to be ongoing. An example would be a gratitude affirmation for improved focus, concentration or stress relief at the workplace. The Infinity symbol is also supportive when you would like to rewrite the energy of a past wrong that you feel may be holding you back. The infinity symbol can travel anywhere through the space-time continuum. This ancient symbol is most commonly used to represent a state of balance and give and take between opposing forces. This is a fantastic symbol to use when working with the cosmos, angelics, and star beings.

Diamond

The shape of the diamond best represents clarity, brilliance, and wisdom. Diamonds themselves are one of the best natural mediums for reflecting light. This symbolic energy is ideal for grids where you want to shed more light on a situation or bring in more clarity and insight. This shape also represents a balance of power.

Many natives of the Americas use the diamond shape to represent the butterfly, transformation, and immortality. This can also be used when seeking new adventures, experiences, directions, and paths. The diamond shape can also be symbolic of purity and clarity.

The Greeks call the shape a Rhombus; which means something round that spins. They refer to a solid rhombus as two circular cones that share the same base or foundation. This is an ideal shape to use to keep together family, friends, and couples that are moving in opposite directions.

Spiral

Spirals are very mystical and represent a wide variety of ways energy can be on the move. They most commonly represent the outward and inward journeys of the soul or the movement of linear time from past to future as it spirals out. This is an ideal shape to use when you want to bring about growth in new directions, transformation and creative energy that keeps flowing deeper inward or expanding outward.

The spiral also represents an unfolding and the process of self-opening; making it the perfect shape to use in grids where you want to manifest windows of opportunity opening up for you. This movement can also symbolize the once hidden revealing itself. It's a potent design for divination and is most likely why it was used to induce a state of hypnosis for the purposes of revealing what the subconscious has hidden.

Counterclockwise spirals move energy out, and clockwise spirals draw energy in. This is important to know if you have a spiral working to draw energy in or away from a focus piece.

THE ART OF CRYSTAL GRID MAKING

Crop Circles

Crystal alchemy grids that are inspired by famous crop circles and their unusual designs can bring in the energy of the cosmic self or a "reaching for the stars" potential. These are like a picture that is worth a thousand words. If you have a calling to reach out to the multi-verse and back, experiment with these phenomenal designs. An example would be any healing work related to the ages of time, celestial cycles and passages, multi-dimensions, or star family.

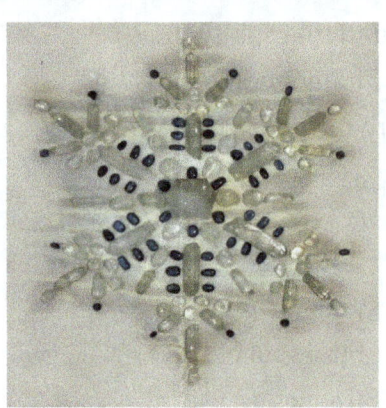

Snowflakes

You may find your greatest inspiration here. No two are alike, so there are infinite ideas to draw inspiration from when studying the shapes of snowflakes. These are exceptionally suited for grids bringing goodwill to something extra special, like a wedding celebration grid, new baby congratulations grid, graduation from college grid, etc. I also appreciate them for being nature made by the original artist of creation itself.

Stars and Starbursts

Stars most commonly represent fame, success, good fortune, and good luck. It can also represent high aspirations, achievements, and ideals. Creating a starburst radiates this energy out further. Spiraling a starburst takes the energy multi-dimensional, and can add the properties discussed of the spiral.

Special note - There is a wide variety of meaning within religious and occult texts related to stars and the number of points they have and their orientations, making it a subject that falls beyond the scope of this guide.

CHAPTER SIX

Free-forms

Let creative free play and intuition be your guides. With free-forms you can become a storyteller. For example, say that your gratitude affirmation is for support while breaking a habit. You can create a repetitive series of dots (the habit) and then break it open with curling waves leading to photos of what would bring you more freedom, peace, and joy as your reward for keeping disciplined.

You can create a design of circles with openings if your goal is to join groups or communities. Place a special piece inside that represents yourself. If you want to gain greater control over a situation, you can bring a wavy line straight that ends inside of a square or a circle. It's creating a map for the energy to follow.

You can create abstract, asymmetrical, designs that create interesting directions of movement, such as the example on the upper right hand of this page. Asymmetry creates a visual sense of "curiosity." Working with odd numbers of crystals also stimulates energy.

Your crystal alchemy grids will take on new dimensions if you play with free-forms and even leave small openings in otherwise closed forms like circles, triangles, and squares. These small openings work well when you wish to "break free" into something new.

It is worthwhile to step back and notice how you "feel" when looking at your creations. Make adjustments until you feel the energy of alchemical transformation moving you into a higher state. When you enjoy being in your grid's presence and have no more desire to move pieces around or switch them out for other pieces is when the alchemical magic begins.

Chapter Seven

Cleansing Energy Fields

Cleansing your crystals, and yourself, before working with them is very important. Crystals and stones do so much for us in part because of their ability to neutralize discordant energies and to receive activation programming. If their aura is not cleansed prior to a new use, or during prolonged use, the crystals and stones start to lose their ability to absorb energetic smog. This pollution leaves them unable to neutralize energy or receive and transmit any activation programming. They can become dull feeling and go dormant without regular cleansing.

Crystals That Self Cleanse

Some crystals and stones are said to be self-cleansing. I still cleanse them all. The act of cleansing your crystals and stones always feels good. When working with energy fields, practicing healthy energetic hygiene is critical for getting results and for your wellbeing. I feel that Selenite comes close to having self-cleansing properties. I keep various pieces of Selenite around my other crystals to keep them more vibrant. It pays to work Selenite into grids that will be ongoing; such as when setting a general ambient field in a room or at the office.

When incorporated into any of your crystal alchemy grids, Selenite will keep the field free of any accumulated energetic smog. Even if your affirmations are for bringing more joy

Photo at left - "Mastering Manifestation Activation" Stilbite tumbleds, Sunstone tumbleds, Clear Quartz pyramids and double terminated points, Selenite spheres, Copper spheres and pendulum points on quartz crystal sand.

into the life of someone a thousand miles away, the crystals may absorb subtle energetic smog through the quantum field that may be interfering with the person's ability to experience improved well-being. I cannot think of an aim that would not benefit from some amount of absorbing energetic smog in order to bring about shifts in the ambient energy that generate improvements.

Methods For Cleansing Crystals

Singing Bowl or Tuning Fork Sound Waves

The tones that come from Tibetan and crystal singing bowls, tuning forks and even chimes gently break up the energy of a discordant and dense field, allowing for a release of the energy to vibrate back into its natural hertz frequency. Sound waves are my favorite cleansing tool.

Vocal Toning from the Heart

Our voices are powerful toners and tuners of energy and can work very well to disperse fields

of energetic smog and density. To keep it simple, tone the sound of the heart chakra, which is the sound of "Ahhhh". Focus on your heart center, and bring your thoughts and feelings into alignment with purity, unconditional love, and Universal wisdom. This can be a very effective method when other more stable tones and methods are not available.

Visual White Light Projection and Envelopment from the Heart

You can use some alchemical magic by imagining your crystals and body being bathed in a field of pure Divine white light. Throw in a dash of charm by adding golden sparks or rainbow shimmers to the white light. If you have a good imagination, this method is extremely effective and ideal.

Sage, Palo Santo Holy Wood, and Incense

Wafting the smoke through any crystal or stone with the aim of cleansing energy works very well. You can also burn incense to infuse the smoke into the energy of the grid. Pure alchemy! Don't forget to include yourself.

Plant Essence, Oils, and Spray Mists

This is one of my favorite methods. Not only is it easy, but I just love the feel of the synergy when the plant and mineral crystal kingdoms come together in the dance of a misting cleanse. This method brings a burst of refreshment to your psyche as well. Any natural essential oil will work well for this. You can make your spray solution with one drop of essential oil per 2 ounces of water. Add three drops of a silver solution or alcohol for a preservative if you will not be using it often. I recommend brown or cobalt glass bottles when creating essential oil mists.

I will mist a grid maybe once every three days. I also like to use oil warmers to diffuse the essences into the grid's energy. It's nice to light them in the evenings.

Moon Light

Using the moon for a crystal and stone cleansing is worth the effort when you are working with crystals and grids for self-reflection during phases of rapid growth and transition. The moon does impart its own light codes that support of this. The moon's gentle light makes it safe for crystals that would fade in the sun such as Amethyst and Celestite.

Sun Light

I do bring some out into the sun periodically though for different reasons. When you have dozens to hundreds and, perhaps some may have thousands of pieces, it would become quite the chore. Thankfully, there are so many alternative methods for cleansing their auric fields right where they sit. If I do bring any crystals out into the sun, it may be for programming from the sun itself. The sun is emitting its own light codes that program our crystals related to the ascension of Gaia and for those choosing to ascend with her.

Cleaning the Stones and Crystals of Debris

A gentle rinsing with a mild soap, fresh water, and a baby soft toothbrush, followed by an immediate drying with a soft towel or hair dryer should do the job for *polished* crystals only. Caution though, a few *raw crystals*, like Aragonite clusters and Pink Kunzite, can dissolve quickly in water and break apart. I know many worry about their Selenite pieces and water exposure. I have accidentally left Selenite out in the rain overnight, and they were fine. It takes soaking them submerged in water for a few weeks before they start to dissolve. I know because I left one in my pool. If any have a musty smell from microscopic mold growth, you can add some borax powder found in the laundry cleaning section of any store to the mild soap solution, mist with some silver solution or dry them out in the sun. I use an ozone generator.

Once they have been physically cleaned they usually only require a regular dusting off. For crystals with clusters of points, you can use the soft brush attachment of your vacuum cleaner, a soft paintbrush or a soft toothbrush to get into the crevices. For your smooth stones and tumbled pieces, you can gently wipe with a damp or dry cloth.

CHAPTER SEVEN

Special Note on Water and Saltwater

Many people suggest bathing crystals in salt water to cleanse them. Saltwater can put your crystals at risk of fracture. I had it happen, and it was a sad discovery. Because of so many other viable methods to choose from, I don't find it necessary to take the risk.

Chapter Eight

Creating Your Crystal Alchemy Grids

It can take several years of dedicated research to learn and memorize all of the metaphysical properties of dozens to hundreds of crystals, stones, and metals; as well as essential oils, symbolism, the laws of attraction and manifesting, the metaphysics of crystal gridding, some basic principles of metaphysics and so much more. All of this specific research has been done for you. Now that you know the history, the basics of creating active and sustaining energy fields for crystal grid manifesting, you can draw specific choices and inspiration from the two following guides. Once you have read the book, and refer to the guides if needed, you will be amazed with yourself and your new crystal grid creations and the results if practiced as taught.

The gratitude affirmations guide here in Chapter 8 (page 67) gives you a place to start with. You can look at the governing areas and find the field of gratitude that you wish to manifest within. Follow any of the suggestions for creating your custom grid. If you own crystals and stones that are not suggested, you can reference the color palette listed for each field of gratitude. The color palettes and guide let you know which colors of crystals and stones best support which fields of gratitude. Everything in this book is here for your quick and easy reference. If at any point your intuition, resources or personal knowledge lead you to deviate, follow that feeling first and foremost!

Photo at left - "Divine Symphony Alignment Activation Code" Apophyllite tips, Turquoise tumbleds, Arkansas Lemurian Seed crystals, Copper tubes and written Language of Light code.

Ready to Start Creating!

Once you have your field of gratitude selected, you can begin gathering your materials with gratitude held in your heart. Use your imagination to visualize the pictures of what you are aiming at to manifest. This, while feeling as if it is already happening, is an important pre-activation step. Once you have gathered your crystals it is a good practice to begin with cleansing yourself, crystals and grid space by following the instructions starting on page 58. We are working with subtle energies and fields. Any distortions in these fields can create resistance. We want to clear the road so to speak. When you have finished creating your design, state the gratitude affirmation to activate the program for the grid. Feel free to customize it for specificity. It's more powerful to say it aloud. Stay in your heart, and feel trust and appreciation for what is being made manifest in the affirmative now.

"A truly thankful heart will bring light into your life and peace into your soul." Anonymous

Special Note—If you are creating a crystal alchemy grid to affect change for another person, it's important to either ask for their permission if this is possible or affirm that positive transformation may take place only if aligned with the integrity of their soul purpose. This will help to open the way for the action to cause a shift in their energy field. Respect for the free will and the soul path of others is everything in a civilized and respectful Universe. It can otherwise create control issue karmic bonds between you and the other person. Believe me, you do not want that. If they wouldn't want it for themselves, do not wish it for them or you will become entangled. Always remember that what we wish for others, we wish for ourselves. What we put out into the multi-verse comes back tenfold so be mindful of this. Whatever it is we do in life, if we do it including that it be for the greatest and highest good of all, we can keep ourselves free and clear of any karmic entanglements. It simply feels good to do too!

Photo at right - "Return of Light" Winter Solstice. Quartz standing point arrangement inspired by Stonehenge, Clear quartz points to radiate the energy and design inspired by the ice crystals of a winter snow, snow quartz for 'frozen light" eternal light symbolism, heat treated Citrine, Pyrite, candles; to symbolize the light and Moss cloth.

CHAPTER EIGHT

Fields of Gratitude

"Gratitude in advance is the most powerful creative force in the universe. "
Neale Donald Walsch

How to Use Them

The fields of gratitude titles on the following pages are broadly based to include everything you could imagine to manifest. I give them this name "fields of gratitude" to help others see it the way I do. We are truly blessed with the abundance of the Universe and it is when we are within gratitude that receiving begins to become more regular and seemingly effortless. When in gratitude, we feel good and all labor is more joyful. Before we can become conscious co-creators, able to shift the energy of our experiences in alignment with our higher potentials, we need to be clear vessels ourselves. It starts with choosing to be in a grateful heart, mind, body, and soul. (page 21)

The fields of gratitude guide gives you suggestions for crystals, stones, and metals to use. You can choose from any of them or use any that you have that are not mentioned if their color is suggested in the color palette. I put the crystals and stone recommendations into three separate general, yet rough price points, to help with budgeting and relative ease of finding them when planning on making new purchases. (page 27)

Symbols hold the power from everyone who has ever invested the high value of their belief in them. Using them is an easy way to amplify the power of attraction in your field of potential. Sacred geometry naturally lends supportive energy straight from the intelligence of the Creator. If any symbols hold special meaning and value to you, I suggest using them. What is personal to us holds a lot of power within our lives, good or bad. (page 30)

Complimentary items are suggested for incorporating into your designs. They have been specially chosen to help support the specific field of gratitude that you are working with.

Photo at left - Rhodochrosite, Golden Tiger Eye, and Tiger Iron tumbleds formed in the popular Gratitude symbol.

This includes diffusing or misting essential plant oils into the grid field. This act intensifies the synergy with the mineral and crystal kingdoms. Their natural purity helps to keep the auric field clear. Their frequencies also work directly to support the affirmation, such as if using a tree oil for supporting affirmations for manifesting stability during a rocky passage or Chamomile for supporting affirmations for manifesting gentility and comfort. (page 34)

Musical notes and vocal toning sounds are suggested for those who wish to use sound wave vibrations to further amplify and support the energy in the field of gratitude. These notes will also help to keep the auric field clean and strong when generated regularly. (page 58)

There is a reminder to incorporate focus pieces if they apply because they truly help. Energy flows where attention goes. These pieces better hold the focus of the affirmation active in the field of gratitude. (page 33)

Finish with activating your grid by stating the gratitude affirmation provided. Feel free to customize for specificity. Make sure to include gratitude, speak in the affirmative now, and include for the greater good of all. Whether you keep them simple or create more elaborate grids by using compliments, focus pieces, sacred geometry, creative layout boards, essential oils, and sound wave energy, it's all good when in a grateful heart. If you feel you have nothing to be grateful for, start with the fact that you are breathing and can read. Both abilities are highly valued in this world. "Giving thanks for the breath of life and ability to read!"

Give yourself the freedom to play. Move elements around. Take some away if they do not "feel" right. Add others that just make more sense to you, even though they may not be suggested. You will develop greater intuitive ability if you spend time 'feeling" different designs and combinations. Ask others how your grids make them feel. This feedback helps.

There may be a tendency if you are new to gridding to use every crystal and stone that you own. I suggest making it a habit to practice editing out some pieces when you think you are done, especially if you are new to this. When it doubt, work with groups of no more than three colors. Once I have created a grid, I walk away from it for a while and come back to it. I usually see and feel where I can make some changes to really feel the alchemical magic kick in.

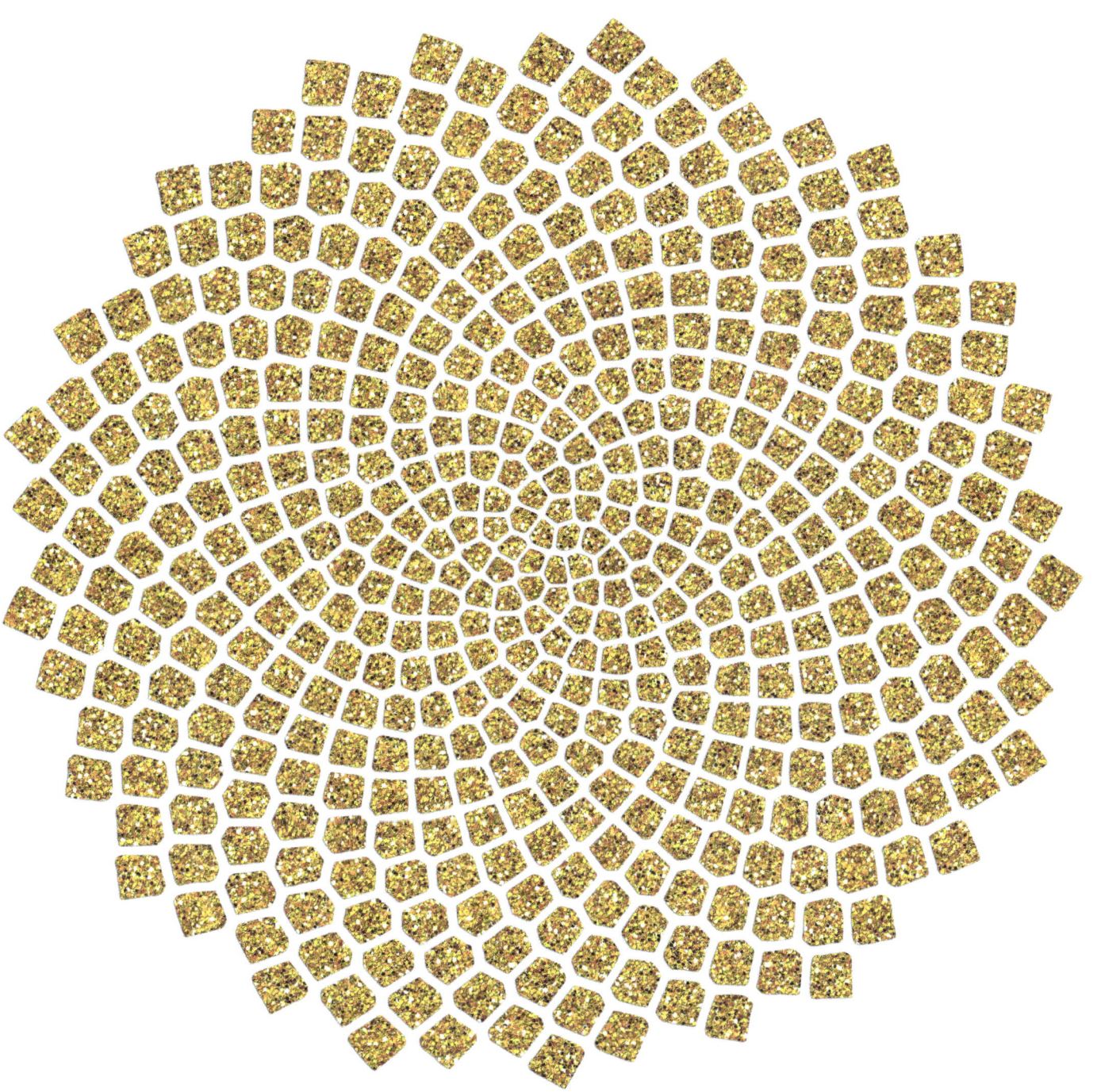

Photo above– Golden Ratio

CHAPTER EIGHT

Joy

Good Cheer, Optimism, Happiness, Enthusiasm, Gratitude, Universal Love, Celebration, Positivity, and Confidence

"Optimism is knowing that you will be okay no matter what." Oprah Winfrey

"They say a person needs just three things to be truly happy in this world: someone to love, something to do, and something to hope for." Tom Bodet

Gratitude Affirmation Activation

"Giving thanks for the states of happiness, positivity, and optimism that I am enjoying with great ease and in good spirits, for the greatest good of all. Giving thanks to the crystal wisdom keepers for their Divine service to this affirmation. And so it is." ~ from the heart

Color Pallet - Yellow, Orange, Green, Rainbow, Purple, Copper, Silver or Gold

Common $ Citrine, Orange, Yellow and Green Calcite, Yellow Jasper, Clear Quartz, Rainbow Quartz, Fire Agate, Bloodstone, and Amethyst

Nice Find $$ Amazonite, Sunstone, Turquoise, Tumbled Emerald, Pyrite, Pink Opal, Chrysocolla, Yellow/Golden Labradorite, and Copper

Rare $$$ Emerald, Dioptase, Spirit Quartz, Sugilite, Peridot, Gold, and Silver

Geometry
  Simple - V shape and Diamond
  Creative - Starbursts, Spiraling Star Bursts, and overlapping Diamonds over Circles, and Flower of Life

Compliments - Flowers in general, especially Daisies, Tiger Lily, Marigold, Sunflowers and Sun Flower Seeds; Exotic Fruits, Pieces of Sweet Candy, Vibrant Feathers, Bright Silken Fabrics, and Dried Spices Like Anise Seed

Essential Oils or Incense - Citrus Oils, especially Red Mandarin, Sweet Orange, Cinnamon, Peppermint, Lemon, Cardamom, Bergamot, Jasmine, Sandalwood, Vanilla, and Wild Violet

Governing Sound Frequency - Musical Notes D, F, and G
Vocal Toning Sound - "Vahm", "Yahm", and "Hahm"

Add your personal focus pieces if you wish. See page 33.

Insights - For both of these sample grids it was important to use bright colors as they are known for raising energy and lifting spirits. Bright colors are a compliment key for shifting the energy in this field of gratitude. I didn't use a metal in the "Celebration" grid because the Amethyst cluster is on its matrix which helps to hold the energy stable. The natural grasses that make up the basket weave, which I used for the layout board, along with the flowers, leaves, and wood flooring, also all work to stabilize the field into the earth plane. Many natural elements from nature such as these, especially crystals still on their matrix, can act as your frequency field stabilizers. In the scrapbooking section of your local arts and crafts store, you can find fun things to incorporate into your grid, making it feel very festive and playful in support of this field of gratitude. I highly recommend creating them as visual displays for adding sparkle to any festive occasion or celebration!

Photo on page 70 - "Cheer" Clear Quartz amplifying the bright colors of the rainbow on a white marble tile and the silver rings help stabilize the field of potential.

Photo at the right - "Celebration" Amethyst cluster, standing points, mini spheres and tumbleds, Tangerine Rose Quartz, Tangerine Aura tumbleds, Clear Quartz standing points, pyramids and pendulum points, Orange Calcite beads, Ice Quartz tumbleds, and orange Lilies with greens from the garden.

CHAPTER EIGHT

Safety

Protection, Security, Courage, Empowerment, Confidence, Anxiety, Preparedness, and Foresight

"The best protection anyone can have… is courage." Elizabeth Cady Stanton

"There are only two kinds of people who can drain your energy: those you love, and those you fear. In both instances it is you who let them in. They did not force their way into your aura, or pry their way into your reality experience." Anthon St. Maarten

Gratitude Affirmation Activation

"Giving thanks for the state of being safe, feeling: protected, strong and brave, with the greater good of all involved. Giving thanks to the crystal wisdom keepers for their Divine service offered to this affirming action. And so it is." ~ from the heart

Color Pallet - Black, Red, Earth tones, Bronze or any metal substitute. For heart protection, add greens. For psychic protection add purples. For social protection add yellows. For protection from electronic smog be sure to include black, especially Shungite. For protection from negative energy make sure to use black and blue if you do not have a Smoky Quartz in the grid.

Special note - *If this is a field of gratitude you may be working with regularly, I highly suggest investing in Black Kyanite Blade for mending tears and holes in the auric field.*

Photo on page 74 - "Security" Clear Quartz standing points and points, Tiger Eye, Smoky Quartz and Black Tourmaline tumbleds and Red Aragonite Clusters for cleansing negativity and worry, Garnet, Ruby and Red Aventurine tumbleds for security, Green Sardonyx tumbleds for security of health and wealth, Hematite rounds and pendulums for field stabilization. Quartz angel figurine keeps a guardian watch over the focus field.

Common $ Black Tourmaline, Amethyst, Tiger Eye, Red Aventurine, Smoky Quartz and Hematite

Nice Find $$ Black Kyanite Blade, Black Onyx, Lapis Lazuli, Rutilated Quartz, Petrified Wood, Shungite, Malachite, Angelite, Pyrite, Blue Apatite, Bronzite, Labradorite, Red Aragonite Star Cluster, Garnet, Purple Fluorite and Arfvedsonite (aka Astrophyllite)

Rare $$$ Herkimer Diamond, Sugilite, Spirit Quartz, Ruby, and Azurite

<u>Geometry</u>
  Simple - Circles, Pyramids, Diamonds, and Squares
  Creative - Overlapping Diamonds, Infinity Symbol, and Tiered

Compliments - Orgone Generators, River Stones, Keys, Shields, Hearts, and Towers

Essential Oils or Incense - White Angelica, Sage, Sandalwood, Dragons Blood (It's a flower), Cedar Atlas, Rosemary, Patchouli, Pine, and Eucalyptus

Governing Sound Frequency - Musical Notes C, E and A

Vocal Toning Sound - "Auhm", "Rahm" and "Shahm"

Add your personal focus pieces if you wish. See page 33.

Insights - Symbolism played a powerful role in the example "Protection" grid to the right. I placed "sticks and stones" symbolic of the things bullies throw our way, outside of the field of protection; keeping all inside of it safe. I added a mini dream catcher key chain that I came across to support peaceful sleep from nightmares. We always feel safe in the love of others which is why I chose to create the grid around the heart shape Blue Apatite stone. Sage smudge was added to the design to symbolize keeping negative energy away.

Photo at right - "Restore Power" Lapis Lazuli for psychic protection and power, Bronzite and Pyrite for power, Blue Apatite for healing emotional trauma, heat treated Citrine and Orange Calcite for confidence and personal empowerment, Petrified Wood (for protection from the Ancestors) and Herkimer Diamond for cohesion.

CHAPTER EIGHT

Stability

Balance, Security, Strength, Power, Responsibility, Organization, Order

"Life is like riding a bicycle. To keep your balance, you must keep moving."
Albert Einstein

"The humble are the most stable in life." Anonymous

"Passion is energy. Feel the power of focusing on what excites you." Oprah Winfrey

Gratitude Affirmation Activation

"Giving thanks for the experience of being stable and balanced in my greatest power which I am utilizing for the greater good of all. Giving thanks to the crystal wisdom keepers for their Divine service offered to this affirming action. And so it is." ~ from the heart

Color Pallet - Earth tones, Black, Red, Blue, Orange, Green, White, Clear, Charcoal, and Slate

Common $ Any Quartz, any Jasper or Agate, any Calcite, any Sardonyx, Hematite, Pyrite, Carnelian, Black Tourmaline, Sodalite, Unakite, Bloodstone, Apache Tears, Petrified Wood, any Tiger Eye, Amethyst, Moonstone and any Fluorite

Nice Find $$ Selenite, Shungite, Garnet, Labradorite, Lapis Lazuli, Red Aragonite Star Cluster, Scolecite and Green Jade

Rare $$$ Ruby, Silver, Moldavite and Herkimer Diamond

Geometry
    Simple - Square, X Shape, Diamond, and Pyramids
    Creative - Infinity Symbol and Vesica Piscis

Compliments - Yin Yang Symbols, Water Features, Metals, Woods, Squares, Blocks/Cubes, Pine Cones and Branches, Ocean Soundscapes and River Rocks

Essential Oils or Incense - Tree resins and oils lend their energy well to this field of gratitude. Cedar Atlas, Balsam Fir, Eucalyptus, Sandalwood, Patchouli, and Frankincense as stabilizing essential oils.

Governing Sound Frequency - Musical Notes C, D and A
Vocal Toning Sound - "Lahm", "Vahm" and "Shahm"

Add your personal focus pieces. See page 33.

Insights - The unusual shape of the grid on page 81 was inspired by the quote from Albert Einstein, "Life is like riding a bicycle. To keep your balance, you must keep moving." I wanted to use stones that support our stable and empowered movement through life, suggesting a forward direction with the design. The grid design on page 78 is about bringing in the energy of balance. Field stabilizing stones, and metals also give a feel of visual strength and stability.

Photo on page 78 - "Power" Shungite cylinders and beads for stabilizing energy, the cylinder shape is for balance and stability, Labradorite spheres for mental acuity, Clear Quartz pyramids and points for power generation, program directing and energy flow, Golden Labradorite tumbleds for confidence and solar plexus support.

Photo on page 81 - "Stability" Ammonite is symbolic of the golden ratio, the base for everything in creation, Red Jasper, Unakite, Petrified Wood, and Bronzite tumbleds for root chakra support, Clear Quartz chips for power generation and program directing, Pyrite and Black Onyx tumbles for field stability and a symbolic stable foundation.

CHAPTER EIGHT

Well Being

Vitality, Health, Healing, Mending, Reconnection, Caring, Feeling, Support, Gentility, Trust, Kindness, Nurturing, Sensitivity, Communication, and Forgiveness

"Health and cheerfulness naturally beget each other." Joseph Addison

"Don't tell me the moon is shining; show me the glint of light on broken glass."
Anton Chekhov

"The greatest wealth is health." Virgil

Gratitude Affirmation Activation

"Giving thanks for the state of wellbeing and the flow of vital life force energy that is being enjoyed each day, for the greatest good of all. Giving thanks to the crystal wisdom keepers for their Divine service offered to this affirming action. And so it is." ~ from the heart

Color Pallet - Cool Reds and Blues, Greens, Yellows, Pastels, Silver, Gold and Earth Tones

Common $ Citrine, Green Aventurine, Carnelian, Bloodstone, Hematite, Pyrite, Red or Yellow Jasper, Tiger Eye, Amethyst, Rose Quartz, Petrified Wood, and Apache Tears
Nice Find $$ Garnet, Ruby Fuchsite, any Apatite, Red Aragonite Cluster and Prehnite
Rare $$$ Ruby, Phenakite, Silver, Gold, Emerald, Herkimer Diamond, and Petalite

Geometry
　　Simple - Circles, Pyramid, and Diamond
　　Creative - Seed of Life and Fibonacci Spiral

Compliments - Fresh or Dried Herbs, Orgone Generator, Seeds, Candles, Water Fountain, Fresh Fruit and Flowers, Honeycomb, Evergreen Branches, Eucalyptus, and Pine Cones
Essential Oils or Incense - Sweet Orange, Rosemary, Birch, Helichrysum, and Eucalyptus

Governing Sound Frequency - Musical Notes C, E, and F
Vocal Toning Sound - "Lahm", "Rahm", and "Yahm"

Add your focus pieces if you wish. See page 33.

Special note - *Crystals and stones resonate with subtle energy fields and do not directly treat physical diseases. As Einstein and Tesla have said, it is all vibration, frequency, and energy. Our physical health is a manifest reflection of the health in our subtle bodies. So logically, crystals and stones that support our subtle energy fields are thought to be of benefit for any deteriorating health condition we or a loved one may be experiencing.*

Insights - I created the "Emotional Wellbeing" grid on page 82 inside of water to demonstrate an example of water itself, acting as a very powerful amplifier and program director. Water is also symbolic of the emotional body. Fresh cut oranges were used in the "Feel Better Fast" grid on page 85 for its healing symbolism of being loaded with Vitamin C and sunlight. Orgone generators lend vital orgone energy to biological bodies whose energy is in a depleting state. Persons with a disease have a measurably lower Hz frequency; so Orgone is believed to help raise it. Heat treated Citrine was used for support of the solar plexus chakra. It is said that any problem one has can be reduced to a depleted solar plexus chakra. The reasoning is that when we have use of our full power, we can make anything right again with it.

Photo on page 82 - "Emotional Wellbeing" Ruby in Zoisite spheres, Rose Quartz and Prehnite tumbleds for heart chakra healing and support, raw Ruby chips for vitality, Apophyllite tips for pristine energy, and double terminated Clear Quartz points running healing energy into the water bowl (emotional body) from the Quartz Angels.

Photo on page 85 - " Feel Better Fast" Orgone and Clear Quartz pyramids for power generation, Pyrite tumbleds and pendulums and heat treated Citrine points for solar plexus chakra support, Apophyllite tips for raising energy, fresh cut orange slices for the symbolic healing energy of Vitamin C and a healing Himalayan salt lamp.

CHAPTER EIGHT

Creativity

Movement, Passion, Inspiration, Play, Self Expression, Artistic Expression

"Creativity is allowing yourself to make mistakes. Art is knowing which ones to keep."
Scott Adams

"Art is the immortal movement of its time." Karl Marx

Gratitude Affirmation Activation

"Giving thanks for the creative energy flowing through me and out into my passions for the greater good of all. Giving thanks to the crystal wisdom keepers for their Divine service offered to this affirming action. And so it is." ~ from the heart

Color Pallet - Copper, Bronze, White, and all others except for Black

Common $ Moonstone, Carnelian, Orange Calcite, Rainbow Quartz, Amethyst, Fire Agate, Rutilated Quartz, Citrine, and Red Jasper

Nice Find $$ Sunstone, Blue Apatite, Amazonite, Scolecite, Copper, Garnet, tumbled and rough Ruby, Turquoise, Chrysocolla, Bronzite, Copper, and Opal

Rare $$$ Ruby, Ajoite, Gold, and Sugilite

Geometry
    Simple - Star and Star Burst
    Creative - Spirals, Seed of Life, Phi, Fibonacci Spiral, Spiral Starburst, Spray burst, Vesica Piscis, Fractal Art, Crops Circles, Abstract, and Tiered

Compliments - Unusually shaped crystals, paint brushes, colored pencils, musical notes, textured fabrics, clay, many of the same item in different sizes of scale, and any element from nature

Essential Oils or Incense - Sweet Orange, Cinnamon, Vanilla, Violet, Grapefruit, Clove, and Sandalwood

Governing Sound Frequency - Musical Notes D and G
Vocal Toning Sound - "Vahm" and "Hahm"

Add your personal focus pieces if you wish. See page 33.

Insights - The "Artistic Inspiration" grid on page 86 utilizes the symbolism of paint brushes to bring in supportive energy from all the artists that have ever brought paint to canvas. Orange is a predominant color to support the sacral chakra which governs our creative beingness. The white pieces symbolize the blank canvas ready to receive the colors of creation (symbolized in the silver star pieces). The tiered and layered grid on page 89 is about the movement of inspired energy. Using a candle holder as a foundation for a grid in itself lends the energy of interest for inspiring unusual ideas. The pink and aqua stones used in the "Inspiring Movement" grid on page 89 are meant to stimulate our high heart intuitive center for Divine inspiration.

Photo on page 86 - "Creative Stimulation" Orange Tangerine Aura Quartz cluster for the power generator and director and tumbleds to support the Sacral chakra. Clear Quartz tumbleds for more power generation to the field. Silver stars for field stability, filled with gem colors for the symbolism of a painters color palette. Scolecite wands and tumbleds for the symbolic blank canvas and tapping higher inspirational states. Swarovski crystals for the energy of magical sparkle and paint brushes as supportive compliments.

Photo on page 89 - "Inspiring Movement" Clear quartz standing point, points, hanging pendulums and tumbleds for power generation, program directing and movement of energy. Rhodochrosite, Rose Quartz and Larimar tumbleds for stimulating the high heart chakra. White Calcite for tapping the Divine and Golden Tiger Eye for lower creative chakra stimulation.

CHAPTER EIGHT

Success

Ambition, Career, Motivation, Confidence, Passion, Good Fortune, Persistence, Victory, Empowerment, Opportunity, Fulfillment, Achievement, Practice, Perseverance, Dedication, Focus, Reward, and Goals

"To laugh often and love much...to appreciate beauty, to find the best in others, to give one's self...this is to have succeeded." Ralph Waldo Emerson

"Success is nothing more than a few simple disciplines practiced every day." Jim Rohn

"Abundance is a state of mind. When you are living in the state of appreciation, you attract more things to be thankful for." Anonymous

"It is not in the pursuit of happiness that we find fulfillment. It is found in the happiness of the pursuit." Denis Waitley

Gratitude Affirmation Activation

"Giving thanks for the fulfilling experience of achieving success and creating opportunities for myself and for the greater good of all with others. Giving thanks to the crystal wisdom keepers for their Divine service offered to this affirming action. And so it is." ~ from the heart

Color Pallet - Red, Orange, Yellow, Green, Vivid Blue, Violet, and Gold

Common $ Carnelian, Amethyst, Fire Agate, Citrine, any Tiger Eye, Jade, Green and Red Aventurine, Sodalite, Red Jasper, Purple Fluorite, Copper, Rutilated Quartz, Bloodstone, and Pyrite

Nice Find $$ Ruby Zoisite, Sunstone, Yellow/Golden Labradorite, tumbled Ruby, tumbled Em-

erald, Prehnite, Arfvedsonite (aka Astrophyllite), Lapis Lazuli, Blue Apatite, Turquoise, Malachite, Bronzite, Ruby Fuchsite, Aragonite Star Cluster, and tumbled Garnet
Rare $$$ Ruby, Herkimer Diamond, Azurite, Moldavite, Dioptase, Gold, Silver, and Sugilite

Geometry
    Simple - Oval, Pyramid, Diamond, and V for Victory
    Creative - Seed of Life, Phi, Spirals, Vesica Piscis, Tiered, Interlocking Diamonds, Stars, Starbursts, Infinity Symbol, and Vesica Pisces layout board with a smaller grid in the center

Compliments - Orgone Generators, Water Fountains, Keys, Fresh Fruits, and Flowers, Tiny Gifts, Coins, Medals, Jewelry, Fire and Candles, Daffodils, Pyramids, Stars, Peppers, and Mints

Essential Oils or Incense - Sweet Orange, Red Mandarin Orange, Lemon, Cinnamon, Ginger, Cardamom, Clove, Vanilla, Violet, Bergamot, Rose, Frankincense, Sandalwood, and Myrrh

Governing Sound Frequency - Musical Notes C, E, F, and A
Vocal Toning Sound - "Lahm", "Vahm", "Yahm", and "Shahm"

Add your personal focus pieces if you wish. See page 33.

Insights - The "Treasure Map" grid on page 90 was inspired by symbols for obtaining treasure, for the treasure itself with the chest and an X marking the spot. The "Victory" grid on page 93 uses a symbolic V for Victory and a water feature to symbolize the flow of success.

Photo on page 90 - "Treasure Map" Ammonite for creative energy, Clear quartz pyramid power generator and director. Ruby, Golden Tiger Eye, Malachite and Yellow Calcite for good luck and fortune. Heat treated Citrine and Pyrite to symbolize gold treasure, Arfvedsonite (also known as Astrophyllite) wands as field stabilizers.

Photo on page 93 - "Victory" Apophyllite Tips and Stilbite for uplifting energy, Green Aventurine and Pyrite tumbleds for good fortune and field stabilization, Orange Calcite for success, Clear Quartz tumbleds and pendulum points for power generation and directing. A water fountain compliment.

CHAPTER EIGHT

Freedom

Adventure, Release, Letting Go, Change, Opportunity, Change Renewal, New Beginnings, Fresh Starts, Excitement, Play, Light Hearted, Uninhibited, Going Natural, Negative Habit Release

"The essence of pleasure is spontaneity." Germaine Greer

"Live life for the moment. Everything else is uncertain." Louise Tomlinson

Gratitude Affirmation Activation

"Giving thanks for the experience of adventures into the new and yet unexplored that I am enjoying with all whom I meet for the greatest good of all. Giving thanks for the ease at which I can change course and task because of the simple joy it brings feeling free to follow my heart, for the greatest good of all. Giving thanks to the crystal wisdom keepers for their Divine service offered to this affirming action. And so it is." ~ from the heart

Color Pallet - Rich and Bold Earth Tone Colors with Pastel Accents. This a synergy combination of properties for releasing what has been and for opening up to the start of something new.

Common $ Jaspers, Agates, Bronzite, Bloodstone, Unakite, Tiger Eye, Aventurines, and Jade
Nice Find $$ Sunstone, Copper, Malachite, Turquoise, Black Onyx, Lapis Lazuli, and Labradorite
Rare $$$ Gold, Ruby, and Azurite

Geometry
    Simple- X, Star Burst, Arrow, Open Circle, and Spiral

THE ART OF CRYSTAL GRID MAKING

Creative - Star Bursts, Star Burst Spirals, Flower of Life, Tiered, Abstracts, and Crop Circles

Compliments - Water Features, World Map for a Layout Board, Feathers, and Keys

Essential Oils or Incense - Any Spice; especially Ginger, Red Mandarin, Rose, and Sandalwood

Governing Sound Frequency - Musical Note C#, E, F, and A#

Vocal Toning Sound - "Auhm", "Rahm", "Yahm", and "Ahng"

Add your personal focus pieces. See page 33.

Insights - The "Free Spirit" grid on page 94 was inspired by Native American culture and their use of Turquoise to connect them with the Great Spirit. The use of feathers in this grid is tapping into the symbolic energy of being able to "fly away freely". Copper was used in both grids for its dual action ability to stimulate the movement of energy while holding fields of potential stable. In the "New Beginnings" grid on page 97, the complimentary use of seeds is the key. Anything with the symbolic energy of a seed will amplify the energy of new growth in one's life. The use of Orange Calcite is also a powerful choice; as the color stimulates the sacral chakra. This chakra is where we were connected to the umbilical cord. This chakra governs the flow of new life force energy into the creation of our being, bringing new life in physical form. Clearly, the governing power of Orange is a miracle maker!

Photo on page 94 - "Free Spirit" Scolecite wands and Turquoise tumbleds for tapping the energy of the Spirit self, Sunstone for the joy of true being, Clear Quartz standing point for power generation and program directing, Copper for empowerment of self expression and field stabilization and feather compliments for the freedom to fly high.

Photo on page 97 - "New Beginnings" Orange Calcite for stimulating the Sacral chakra connection to the Source of new life. Unakite for enhancing the ability to envision the new and the gentle release of blockages to it, Lemurian Seed Quartz for the support of the information it is encoded with. Copper spheres and pendulum points to stimulate the movement of energy, while also holding the field of potential stable. Pumpkin seeds for new beginnings and for some "Cinderella" (transformation carriage ride off into ones dreams) symbolic energy.

CHAPTER EIGHT

Romance

Romantic Love, Romantic Relationships, Mystery, Passion, Excitement, Soul Mates, Twin Flames, Courtship, Sexual Union, Sexual Attraction, Lovers, and Sweet Hearts

"Romance is the golden dust that makes the everyday life glow." Carolyn Gold Heilbrun

Gratitude Affirmation Activation

"Giving thanks for the exhilarating feeling of being swept away in the romance of life itself, and in the mysterious dance with all others, for the greatest good of all. May its charm and effortless grace, sprinkle the glow of its golden dust along my path forever more. Giving thanks to the crystal wisdom keepers for their Divine service offered to this affirming action. And so it is."
~ from the heart

Color Palette - Deep Red, Green, and Pink, Clear, Gold, Copper, Silver, and Platinum (Smoky, Black and White Tones for accenting the energy of mystery and/ or innocence)

Common $ Carnelian, Blood Stone, Moonstone, Smoky Quartz, Sardonyx, Green and Red Aventurine, Rose Quartz, Clear Quartz Crystal, and Mookaite Jasper
Nice Find $$ Jade, Ruby Zoisite, Pearls, Rhodochrosite, Scolecite, Pink Tourmaline, Rhodonite, Green and Pink Tourmaline, Opal, Emerald rough/ tumbled, Garnet rough/tumbled, Ruby rough/tumbled, and Copper
Rare $$$ Star Ruby, Herkimer Diamond, Sugilite, Petalite, Gold, Silver and Platinum

Photo at left - "Romantic Getaway" Red Aventurine, Pearls, Herkimer Diamond, Pyrite, Smoky and Clear Quartz, Fresh Roses.

CHAPTER EIGHT

Geometry
    Simple - Heart, Ring, and Diamond
    Creative - Infinity Symbol, Interlocking Rings, Curly Starburst, Vesica Pisces with two small hearts in the rings, and one large heart in the overlap

Compliments - Hearts, Water Features, Candles, Wine Glasses, Trains, Novels, Poetry, Love Notes, Feather Pens, Red or White Feathers, Rings, Spices, Doves, Jewelry, and Rice
Essential Oils & Incense - Rose, Cinnamon, Ginger, Red Mandarin, Jasmine, Amber, Sandalwood, and Vanilla

Governing Sound Frequency - Musical Notes D, F, and A#
Vocal Toning Sound - "Vahm", "Yahm", and "Ahng"

Add your personal focus pieces. See page 33.

"She lives to see the sun, and feel the wind, and drink the rain." Lord Huron

Photo at left - "Deepening the Love" Rhodochrosite, Rhodonite, Pink Opal, Charoite, Moonstone, Clear Quartz, Apophyllite tips and Silver plate accents. Symbolic key to the heart, heart chakra tuning fork for supporting the field and a Rose oil diffusion.

Photo at right - "Love is in the Air" Emerald, Ruby, Garnet, Apophyllite tips, Swarovski Crystal, Clear Quartz, Pearls and Gold plate accents. Candle light and crystal wine glasses for their symbolic energy. Raw red Ruby chips are in the wine glasses.

CHAPTER EIGHT

Nurturing Love

Support, Caring, Warmth, Maturity, Kindness, Understanding, Forgiveness, Acceptance, Humble Presence, Self Love and Acceptance, Sharing, Gentility, Divine Feminine, Grace, Ease, and Patience

"Forgiveness is the final form of love." Reinhold Niebuhr

"Know when to release pride and turn to others for support and guidance."
Bear Grylls

"The humble man counts his blessings." Fulton J. Sheen

Gratitude Affirmation Activation

"Giving thanks for the enjoyment of giving and receiving love, and for the warmth of nurturing love and support enjoyed, for the greatest good of all. Giving thanks to the crystal wisdom keepers for their Divine service offered to this affirming action. And so it is." ~ from the heart

Color Pallet - Pinks, Aqua, Greens, Blues, and Browns

Common $ Rose Quartz, Blue Lace Agate, Sodalite, Moonstone, Lapis Lazuli, Calcite - any color, and Fluorite - any color, Petrified Wood (The Ancestors)
Nice Find $$ Pink Tourmaline, Lepidolite, Rhodochrosite, Rhodonite, Prehnite, Emerald, Azurite, Amazonite, Jade, Selenite, Aquamarine, Angelite, and Opal
Rare $$$ Celestite, Sugilite, Stilbite, Larimar, and Pink Kunzite

Photo at left - "Heart Softener" Raw Rose Quartz, Selenite spiral, Rhodochrosite heart, Golden Tiger Eye, Prehnite tumbleds and Clear Quartz points. Heart chakra tuning fork in the note of F and soft, fresh pink Roses.

THE ART OF CRYSTAL GRID MAKING

Geometry
   Simple - Circle and Circle With Rays
   Creative - Snowflake, Phi, and Concentric Circles

Compliments - Herbs, Flowers, Cinnamon Sticks, Ocean soundscape, Eucalyptus Branches, Soft fluffy fabrics and items that feel good to the touch, and Candles

Essential Oils or Incense - Rose, Chamomile, Clary Sage, Lavender, and Frankincense

Governing Sound Frequency - Musical Notes D, F, and G
 Vocal Toning Sound - "Vahm", "Yahm", and "Hahm"

Add your personal focus pieces if you wish. See page 33.

Insights - Music can have a very soothing effect and the use of sound therapy instruments can lend the energetic support to this field of gratitude. Food is also a powerful symbol of something people turn to for comfort. In these sample grids I incorporated both. One has a tuning fork in the note of the heart chakra for love and in the other, I used honey and lemon which can be associated with foods used for soothing when not feeling up to par. A personal favorite for nurturing energy itself is Pink Tourmaline. A softer favorite is Pink Kunzite.

Photo on page 102 - "A Mothers Love" Rhodochrosite for the power of unconditional love, Prehnite for heart healing, Rose Quartz for soft nurturing energy, standing Clear Quartz point and points for power generation and program directing, an angel figurine for the symbolic energy of being watched over by a gentle loving presence. Heart chakra tuning fork for field cleansing, amplifying the affirmation energy, and for field stabilization.

Photo on page 105 - "The Care Giver" Ruby, Rhodonite and Red Aventurine; for vital life force energy and immune system, root chakra support. Heat treated Citrine to bring more active healing energy in to the solar plexus chakra, Smoky Quartz for clearing away "ill energy", double terminated Clear Quartz points for power generation and program directing. Soft compliments of Eucalyptus, Lemon and Honey for their symbolic support in relief from feeling under the weather. The Smoky quartz, wood coaster and Eucalyptus also act as field stabilizers.

CHAPTER EIGHT

Community

Family, Friends, Co-workers, Connection, Unity, Universal Love, Familial Love, Bonding, Trust, Support, Affection, Dignity, Sharing, Education, Leadership, Co-operation, Global and Galactic

"True belonging is born of relationships not only to one another but to a place of shared responsibilities and benefits. We love not so much what we have acquired as much as we love what we have made and whom we have made it with." Robert Finch

"There is not a word yet for old friends who've just met." Jim Henson

"If you go looking for a friend, you're going to find they're very scarce. If you go out to be a friend, you'll find them everywhere." Zig Ziglar

Gratitude Affirmation Activation

"Giving thanks for the enjoyment of life shared with family and friends for the greatest good of all. Giving thanks that we always care to maintain healthy bonds in connection with the greater communities of being. Giving thanks to the crystal wisdom keepers for their Divine service offered to this affirmation action. And so it is." ~ from the heart

Color Pallet - Blue, Orange, Greens, Pinks, and Gold Tones

Common $ Green, Yellow and Orange Calcite, Rose Quartz, Bloodstone, Lapis Lazuli, Blue Lace Agate, Green Aventurine, Green Jade, Petrified Wood, and Carnelian

Nice Find $$ Sunstone, Chrysocolla, Prehnite, Quartz Cluster, Amazonite, Pink Tourmaline, Malachite, Aquamarine, Angelite, Fuchsite, Ruby Zoisite, Ruby Fuchsite, and Opal

Rare $$$ Celestite, Herkimer Diamond, Ruby, Dioptase, Pink Kunzite, and Moldavite

Geometry

Simple - Circle, Infinity Symbol, Diamond, Square, and Heart

Creative - Seed of Life, Lines that Appear Woven, and Repeating Patterns (for tradition)

Compliments - Spheres, Twigs with Leaves (family tree), Smile Faces, Images of Holding Hands and Bridges, Feathers (Birds of a feather flock together), and Hearts

Essential Oils or Incense- Sweet Orange, Spices, Balsam Fir, Cedar Atlas, and Peppermint

Governing Sound Frequency - Musical Notes C#, B, and A#

Vocal Toning Sound - "Auhm" and "Ahng"

Add your personal focus pieces. See page 33.

Insights - In the "Honoring the Roles of the Tribe" grid on page 106, the use of the woven blanket in natural fibers is a supportive compliment, evoking the symbolism of both the tribal community and the weaving of the people that create a community. In the "Warm Gathering" grid to the right, I drew from the symbolism in the popular quote, "birds of a feather flock together" with the use of feathers. Leaves symbolize those connected by a family tree and a candle flame for the symbolic warmth of togetherness when gathering around a fire.

Photo on page 106 - "Honoring the Roles of the Tribe" Rhodochrosite for unconditional love, Turquoise for respect, Garnet for our roots, Ammonites for creation, Lapis Lazuli for wisdom and field stabilization, and Clear Quartz pyramids for program direction and power generation.

Photo on page 109 - "Warm Gathering" Tangerine Aura Rose Quartz and Rose Quartz for warm love, Blue Apatite for deep bonds, Clear Quartz for power generation and program directing, intersecting rings for connecting circles of people, gold leaves and seeds for family connection and field stabilization, feathers of a flock and fire for complimentary warmth.

Purity

Clarity, Forgiveness, Vibrancy, Innocence, Divinity, Cleansing, Renewal and Wisdom

"Purity of speech, of the mind, of the senses, and of a compassionate heart are needed by one who desires to rise to the divine platform." Chanakya

"For me, the greatest beauty always lies in the greatest clarity." Gotthold Ephraim Lessing

" I continue to be drawn to clarity and simplicity. 'Less is more' remains my mantra." Stephane Rolland

Gratitude Affirmation Activation

"Giving thanks for the state of clear, clean and vibrant energy, in a return to my original innocence that I am enjoying, for the greatest good of all. Giving thanks to the crystal wisdom keepers for their Divine service offered to this affirmation action. And so it is." ~ from the heart

Color Pallet - Whites, Rainbow and Clear Quartz, Gold, Silver and Platinum. Bright pastels for field support. Metals, Smoky or Black for absorbing and neutralizing or use a natural material layout board

Common $ Calcite - any color, Clear Quartz, White Quartz, Rose Quartz, Black Tourmaline, Moonstone, Smoky Quartz, Rutilated Quartz, Pearls, Citrine, Rainbow Quartz, Angel Aura, Blue Lace Agate, Amethyst, and Carnelian

Nice Find $$ Selenite, Scolecite, Snow Quartz, Himalayan Quartz, Lepidolite, Shungite, Prehnite, Opal, Pink Opal, and Fluorite - any color

Rare $$$ Herkimer Diamond, Celestite, Spirit Quartz, Stilbite, Gold, Platinum, and Ulexite

Geometry
   Simple - Circle and Diamond
   Creative - Sun with Rays, Vesica Piscis, Spirals, Phi, and Interlocking Diamonds

Compliments - White Feathers, Spheres, Hearts, Candles, Water Feature, Ocean Soundscapes, Flutes, Violins, Crystal Singing Bowl, White Lilies, Angels, Pine Sprigs, Sand, Orgone Generators, and Sea Salt

Essential Oils or Incense - Rose, Helichrysum, Blue Lotus, Lavender, Spikenard, Frankincense, Sandalwood, Myrrh, Lemon, Eucalyptus, Sage, Peppermint, and Pine

Governing Sound Frequency - Musical Notes A and B
Vocal Toning Sound - "Shahm" and "Auhm"

Add your personal focus pieces if you wish. See page 33.

Insights - Candles are a powerful compliment as they provide the symbolism of the cleansing fires of renewal, and the light we can see more clearly with. The "Purity" grid originally had a Selenite lamp where the candle was. I was however moved to switch it to the element of fire and anointing oils. Selenite is used in the "Renewal" grid and is almost a must use crystal for the Purity gratitude field. It brings vibrancy better than any other crystal I have tested. Himalayan salt lamps, salt rocks, and salt itself, are also powerful symbols for purity.

Photo on page 110 - "Purity" Blue Apatite for the symbolic purity in deep oceanic waters, Clear Quartz for power amplification and program direction, heat treated Citrine for transformative fire, Gold plate spheres and rays to symbolize the Radiant light and a Frankincense essential oil diffusion.

Photo on page 113 - "Renewal" Clear Quartz for power amplification and program directing, Selenite and Aquamarine for bringing the energy of cleansing and vibrancy, Himalayan salt lamp and rock for cleansing energy, candle light fire and Lilies for the symbolism of renewal.

CHAPTER EIGHT

Peace

Calm, Serenity, Ease, Understanding, Acceptance, Surrender (Letting go), Tranquility, Forgiveness and Mindfulness

"Feelings are just like having visitors. Let them come and go." Mooji

"I can have peace of mind when I choose to forgive rather than judge." Gerald Jampolsky

"Peace begins with a smile." Mother Theresa

Gratitude Affirmation Activation

"Giving thanks for the state of peace and calm being experienced with all for the greater good of all involved. Giving thanks to the crystal wisdom keepers for their Divine service offered to this affirmation action. And so it is." ~ from the heart

Color Pallet - White, Pink, Light Blue, Any Pastel, and muted Brown Earth Tones

Common $ Quartz Clear, Selenite, Blue Lace Agate, Rose Quartz, Calcite-White and Blue, Apache Tears, Pearl, Unakite, and Petrified Wood
Nice Find $$ Lepidolite, Pink Tourmaline, Pink Opal, Angelite, Snow Quartz, Rhodochrosite, and Aquamarine
Rare $$$ Larimar, Pink Kunzite, Stilbite, Celestite, Spirit Quartz, and Apophyllite

Geometry
    Simple - Circle, Ovals, Balanced or Symmetrical Design, and Horizontal Lines

Creative - Seed of Life, Vesica Piscis, Horizontal Flowing Waves, Interlocking Circles, and Snowflakes

Compliments - Pastel Lush Flowers Like Petunias, Candles or Feathers In Pastel Colors, Angels, Singing Bowls, Chimes, Water Fountain, Ocean Soundscapes, Sea Shells, Pine Sprigs and Cones, Sand, Sea Salt, and Drift Wood

Essential Oils or Incense - Lavender, Sandalwood, Pine, Balsam Fir, Chamomile, Bergamot, Angelica Root, and Patchouli

Governing Sound Frequency - Musical Notes E, F, and G
Vocal Toning Sound - "Rahm", "Yahm", and "Hahm"

Add your personal focus pieces if you wish. See page 33.

Insights - Any natural element found in nature will be a powerful symbolic and energetic compliment to any grid under the gratitude field for Peace. Items from the seashore are generally calming to the visual eye. Pine trees absorb negative energy from us, bringing about a calming effect; so Pine tree sprigs and cones support this field very well.

Photo on page 114 - "Mindfulness" Lapis Lazuli pyramids for balanced and clear perception. Blue Lace Agate tumbleds to calm the soul and emotional body; and for improved mindful being. Smoky Quartz tumbleds for clearing away subtle body pollution that can run interference. Herkimer Diamonds for power amplification, program directing and cohesion. Pyrite tumbleds for field stabilization. Tibetan singing bowl in the note of A for the third eye chakra; which governs mindfulness. Complimentary Pine sprigs and cones for their calming effect.

Photo on page 117 - "Tranquility" Clear Quartz for power amplification and program directing, Larimar for its calming energy, Prehnite for its soothing energy, Blue Kyanite for its peaceful energy, and pearls for the symbolic beauty of what can come from an irritation when it is healed. A water fountain, driftwood, sand and seashells are symbolic compliments to the energy of a tranquil setting.

CHAPTER EIGHT

Spiritual

Cosmic, Celestial, Angelic, Mysticism, Divinity, Psychic, Extrasensory, Meditation, Intuition, Soul Path, Co-Creation, Transformation, Karmic, Imagination, Dreams, Memory, Higher Knowledge, and Star Beings

"There is only one issue: man's lack of experience in feeling his Divine self and his innate connection with the Divine. All other issues stem from this." Lindsay Wagner

"To the mind that is still, the whole universe surrenders." Lao Tzu

"If men were angels, no government would be necessary." James Madison

Gratitude Affirmation Activation

"Giving thanks for the meaningful connection shared with benevolent star, angelic and Spirit family that are always near and dear for support and guidance when needed. Giving thanks to the crystal wisdom keepers for their Divine service offered to this affirmation action. And so it is." ~ from the heart

Color Palette - Platinum, Gold, Silver, White, Rainbow Quartz, Violet, Aqua, Pastels, Clear Quartz

Common $ Unakite, Clear Quartz, White Calcite, Snow Quartz, Rainbow Quartz, Starbraries, Angelite, Petrified Wood, Rutilated Quartz, Rose Quartz, Pearl, Moonstone, Purple Fluorite, and Pearls

Nice Find $$ Apophyllite, Celestite, Arfvedsonite (aka Astrophyllite), Angel Auras, Scolecite, Turquoise, Prehnite, Aquamarine, Lemurian Seed Crystals, Blue Kyanite, and Arkansas Quartz

Rare $$$ Moldavite, Spirit Quartz, Herkimer Diamond, Stilbite, Petalite, and Larimar

Exceptional For This Intention $$$ Ajoite, Stellar Beam Calcite, Sugilite, and Phenakite

Geometry

Simple - Pyramid (trinity)

Creative - Spirals, Overlapping Pyramids, and Star Burst, Crop Circles, Spiraling Star Burst, Wings, and Any Labyrinth

Compliments - Orgone Generator, White Feathers, White or Pastel Flowers, Chimes, Singing Bowls, Kaleidoscopes, Abstract Art, and Animal Spirit Totems. Shells, Sea Glass, and Sand (if the connection being sought is with The Merfolk, Dolphin and Whale Families)

Essential Oils or Incense - Rose, Frankincense, Sandalwood, Patchouli, Lavender, Neroli, Chamomile, Coriander, Violet, Lemon, Jasmine, Red Mandarin, Geranium, and Blue Lotus

Governing Sound Frequency - Musical Notes F and B

Vocal Toning Sound - "Yahm" and "Auhm"

Add your personal focus pieces if you wish. See page 33.

Insights - Use primarily high vibration pieces, clear and white; to help make connections. Pastels are soft with a benevolent feeling. Crystals and stones with metallic rays are very symbolic of Radiant energy; such as Rutilated Quartz and Arfvedsonite (aka Astrophyllite).

Photo on page 118 - "12-12 -1 Portal" Clear Quartz tumbleds for power amplification and program direction, Labradorite for opening psychic awareness, Ammonites for creation codes, Scolecite and White Calcite for tapping open the Spirit/Cosmic self, Selenite for purification to receive, Arkansas Lemurian Seed Quartz to be activated, Ruby for vital life force power, Onyx for field stabilization. A Lemurian Seed Quartz alchemy crystal singing bowl in the note of G# for the ascension point chakra.

Photo on page 121 - "Angelic Light" Tangerine Quartz cluster, clear quartz pyramids, and double terminated points for power amplification and program directing, Fluorite for the energy of higher consciousness, Stilbite for Divine co-creation, Angelite to bring in the angelic energies, and Copper for field stabilization.

Chapter Nine

Governing Colors Guide

"The colors live a remarkable life of their own after they have been applied to the canvas." Edvard Munch

This governing colors guide lets you know where to best use your crystals and stones that may not be suggested in this book. For example, if you have some new Phosphosiderite that you would like to use, refer to the color Pink and what it governs. Your Phosphosiderite will support any gratitude affirmation related to the governing areas of the color pink. Additional information is provided to help you select compliments that will support the variety of color frequencies within your collection when using this beautiful stone. Suggestions for crystals and stones to add to your collection are also given for adding variety to your color palette.

By learning the governing colors, there is no need to have to memorize the vast potential metaphysical properties of hundreds or thousands of crystals and stones. You will be able to work on the spot, and with mastery, by just understanding the power of the color frequency they are generating. Of course, their properties are more complex than this. It's simply an easy yet effective way to get a handle on your collection. For example, if you want to help bring calming energy into a space, you know to select from a blue palette and the supporting compliments for the color blue. If you want to bolster confidence, you know to select from a vivid yellow palette and its supporting compliments. If you are in need of purification, you know that white, black or earth tones will support you best. This will accelerate your adeptness at creating powerful and effective crystal manifestation grids on the spot!

Color Tones Matter

Pastels - Use for sensitive issues that require ease, gentility, nurturing, softness, soothing, and grace. Pastels are beneficial for calming highly aggravated and heated energies.

Vibrant Tones - Use for bringing in more energy, power, stamina, attention, and endurance.

Deep Shades - Use for going more deeply into issues, deep clearing, cleansing, and to bring a sense of safety and stability. Darker colors and tones work like sponges absorbing excess negative, heavy or dense energy. The lighter and pleasant vibrations will escape the pull of the dark stones and crystals leaving a lovely field of natural energy to become predominant, like helium defying gravity. A vibrant color will also help to reinforce the affirmation when also using deep shades or black stones for mopping up any discordant interference.

Light and Clear - Use for uplifting energy, clarity, and Universal purposes. Lighter colors reflect light, increasing the energy output of the grid.

" The color of sound is so definite that it would be hard to find anyone that would express bright yellow with base notes or deep blue with treble."

Wassily Kandinsky

Photo on page 125. I was playing around with a collection of stones for the example of working with the groupings on page 45. I was charmed to created simple grids using just one of a kind to create them. Though many people start off building a collection of just one of a kind, before you start purchasing in groups for more powerful gridding, you can still create very beautiful and interesting crystal alchemy grids. I hope they inspire and encourage you to play with what you have no matter the size of your collection. Rose Quartz kites, Apophyllite tips, Rhodochrosite, Amethyst, Pyrite, Malachite and Lapis Lazuli tumbleds and double terminated points, Rainbow Titanium Aura points, polished Garnet, Clear Quartz tumbleds and Clear Quartz pendulum points were used.

CHAPTER NINE

Shades of Red

Governs

Right to Exist, Survival, Stability, Security, Safety, Strength, Power of Assertion, Steadfastness, Foundations, Financial Security, Abundance, Prosperity, Right Timing, Patience, Bravery, Sexuality (seductive), Passion, Physical Body, Material Existence, Deep Emotions, Seriousness, Stimulates Movement, Elimination, Lymph System, Immune System, Ability to Thrive, and Our Rights to be as we choose to allow others the same freedoms to be.

Crystals, Stones, Minerals, and Precious Metals

Garnet, Ruby, Red Jasper, Red Quartz, Red Aragonite, Red Tiger Eye, Carnelian,

Red Aventurine, and Smoky Quartz

Sound Wave Frequency - Musical Note C

Vocal toning sound - "Auhm" or "Lahm"

Resonant Plant Frequencies

Any Tree, Tree Bark or Root Oil such as Cedarwood, Patchouli, Sandalwood, Eucalyptus,

Lemon, Cinnamon, and Ginger

Resonant Compliments

Squares, Spirals, Phi, Pillars, Red Roses, Metals, Nautilus Shell, Salts, Coins, and Sand

CHAPTER NINE

Shades of Orange

Governs

Vitality, Joy, Creativity, Artistry, Emotional Well-Being and Balance, Healthy Social Interaction, Pleasure, Inspiration, Personal Growth Transformation and Change, Healthy Boundaries, Sexuality (playful), Reproductive Systems, Movement, Grace and Ease, Absorption of Nutrition, and our Rights to Feel and allow others the right to their feelings.

Crystals, Stones, Minerals, and Precious Metals

Orange Calcite, Sunstone, Stilbite, Carnelian, and Copper

Sound Wave Frequency - Musical note D

Vocal Toning Sound - "Vahm"

Resonant Plant Frequencies

Vibrant and/or Unusual and Exotic Fruits, Spices and Florals such as Orange, Cardamom, Clove, Red Mandarin, Violet, Bergamot, Vitex, Ylang Ylang, Jasmine, Sandalwood, and Vanilla

Resonant Compliments

Tiger Lily, Marigold, Orange Fruits, Flowing Water Elements and Features, Feathers, Silken Fabrics, and Spices such as Anise Star

CHAPTER NINE

Shades of Yellow

Governs

Personal Empowerment, Confidence, Will Power, Assertiveness, Spontaneity, Courage, Energy, Moving Forward, Vitality, Goal Achieving, Ambition, Focus, Responsibility, the Ability to Forgive, Digestion, Detoxification, Self Acceptance, Respect for Others, Healthy Personal Boundaries, Reliability, Ability to Meet Challenges, Humor, and the Right to Act while allowing others their rights to go their own way.

Crystal Stones, Minerals, and Precious Metals

Citrine, Golden Tiger Eye, Yellow Calcite, Golden Labradorite, Amber, Bronzite, Pyrite, Gold, and any Metals with Golden Tones

Sound Wave Frequency - Musical Note   E

Vocal Toning Sound - "Rahm"

Resonant Plant Frequencies

Lemon, Frankincense, Cinnamon, Geranium, Peppermint, Black Pepper, Coriander, Ginger, and Cedarwood

Resonant Compliments

Fire and Candles, Dandelions, Black Eyed Susan's, Pyramids, Sun and Stars, Peppers, and Mints

CHAPTER NINE

Shades of Green

Governs

General Well Being, Ability to Trust Others, Personal Stability, Balance, Wealth, Grounded in the Spirit, Self Control, the Flow of Joy, Heart and Lung Function, Shoulders, Arms and Hands, and the Right to Love and Be Loved while allowing others the same.

Crystals, Stones, Minerals, and Precious metals

Green Aventurine, Jade, Malachite, Bloodstone, Ruby Zoisite, Fuchsite, Dioptase, Amazonite, Emerald, and Moldavite (especially if sensitive to solar flares). Moldavite helps to rewire the body to integrate the solar flare energy without disturbance to the vagus nerve.

Sound Wave Frequency - Music Note F

Vocal toning Sound - "Yahm"

Resonant Plant Frequencies

Rose, Lavender, Balsam Fir, Neroli, Spearmint, Frankincense, Eucalyptus, and Sandalwood

Resonant Compliments Feathers, Roses, Doves, Heart Shapes, Interconnected Rings, Leaves, Cherubs, and Angels

CHAPTER NINE

Shades of Blue

Governs

Verbal Communication, Verbal Self Expression and Creativity, Balance, Harmony, Timing and Rhythm, Coolness, Peace, Tranquility, Relaxation, Serenity, Calming, Throat, Neck, Teeth, Gums, Jaws, Ears, and the Right to Speak and to Be Heard while allowing others the same.

Crystals, Stones, Minerals, and Precious Metals

Any Blue Lace Agate (Chalcedony), Sodalite, Angelite, Aquamarine, Celestite, Blue Quartz, Blue Kyanite, Blue Fluorite, Labradorite, Lapis Lazuli, Blue Apatite, and Larimar

Sound Wave Frequency - Musical Note G

Vocal Toning Sound - "Hahm"

Resonant Plant Frequencies

Rosemary, Lemon Eucalyptus, Peppermint, Sage, and Vanilla

Resonant Compliments

Musical Instruments, Sheet Music, Periwinkle, Hydrangea, Written Poetry, Inspiring Quotes, Necklace Jewelry, Flowing Movement in Designs, and Smiley Faces

CHAPTER NINE

Indigo, Violet, and Purple

Governs

Transformation, Perception, Insight, the Balance Between Analytical and Abstract Thought, Trust in the Self, Mental Focus and Concentration, Imagination, Creativity, Memory, Dreams, Mysticism, Soul Path and Life Purpose, Psychic Vision, Brain, Eyes, Sinus, Nose, Endocrine Systems, and the Right to See and Be Seen while allowing others the same.

Crystals, Stones, Minerals, and Precious Metals

Amethyst, Purple Fluorite, Iolite, Labradorite, Sugilite, Lepidolite, and Charoite

Sound Wave Frequency - Musical Note A

Vocal Toning Sound - "Ahng"

Resonant Plant Frequencies

All Tree Oils are Great for Stabilizing, Calming and Balancing Chaotic and Disorderly Thoughts such as Patchouli, Sandalwood, Cedarwood, Pine, Frankincense, Peppermint, and Lemon

Resonant Compliments

Kaleidoscopes, Fractal Art, Orchids, Lilacs, Violets, Windows, Keys, Crowns, Doorways, Mandalas, Symbols of Balance, Vesica Pisces, Infinity Symbol, Clouds, and the Moon

CHAPTER NINE

Aqua and Turquoise

Governs

Assimilation of Spirit into Matter, Universal Peace, High and Low Heart Chakras, Intuition, Emotional Awareness, Universal Acceptance and Forgiveness, Mastery Over the Material Plane, Light Body, Faith, Appreciation, and Atonement

Crystals, Stones, Minerals, and Precious Metals

Aquamarine, Larimar, Turquoise, Aqua Aura, Amazonite, Chrysocolla, Ajoite, and Platinum

Sound Wave Frequency - Musical Note F b and F #, flute

Vocal Toning Sound - "Yahm"

Resonant Plant Frequencies

Ginger, Rose, Lily, Frankincense, Angelica Root, Lemon, Helichrysum, Birch, Sandalwood, and Sage

Resonant Compliments

White Flowers, Green Leaves, Water, Drums, Keys, Bridges, Angels, Arches, and Portals

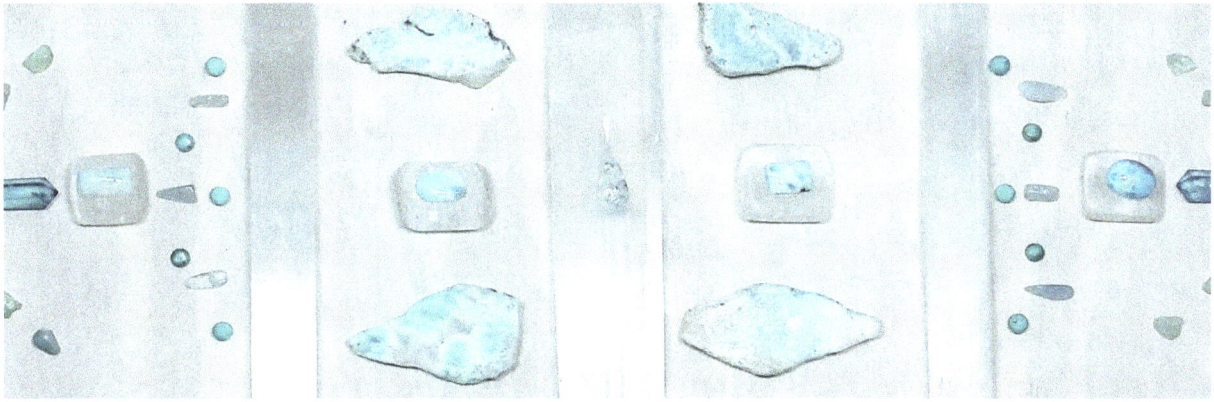

CHAPTER NINE

Shades of Pink

Governs

Nurturing Love, Power in Vulnerability, Softness, Forgiveness, Compassion, Dignity, Understanding, Sweetness, Kindness, Romance, Soothing, Purity of Heart, Honesty, Visibility, Calming, Hope, Trust, Belief, and the Divine Feminine

Crystals, Stones, Minerals, and Precious Metals

Rose Quartz, Rhodochrosite, Lepidolite, Pink Tourmaline, Pink Kunzite, Rhodonite, Pink Opal, Ruby, Silver, and Gold

Sound Wave Frequency - Musical Note F and F#

Vocal Toning Sound - "Yahm"

Resonant Plant Frequencies

Rose, Chamomile, Lavender, Sweet Orange, Balsam Fir, Frankincense, and Eucalyptus

Resonant Compliments

Satin, Silk, Cotton, Infinity Symbol, Chimes, Angels, Quan Yin, Mother Mary, Pearls, Water, Fire, Bamboo, Roses, and Violets

CHAPTER NINE

Rainbow Aura

Governs

Manifesting Throughout the Dimensions, Promises, Hope, Wonder, Awe, Celebration, Cheer, Goodwill, Connections, Bridges, Diversity, Unity, and Mending

Crystals, Stones, Minerals, and Precious Metals

Quartz with Rainbow Inclusions, Rainbow Aura Quartz, Peacock Pyrite, Opal, Moonstones, and Labradorite

Sound Wave Frequency - Musical Note A#, C#, and B

Vocal Toning Sound - "Ahng" and "Auhm"

Resonant Plant Frequencies

Ylang Ylang, Red Mandarin, Lime, Spearmint, and Patchouli

Resonant Compliments

String Instruments, Cosmos Flowers, Rainbows/ Bridges, Spirals, Vesica Piscis, Flower of Life, and Braids

CHAPTER NINE

White

Governs

Awareness, Wisdom, Connection with Universal Self, Spiritual Connection, Consciousness, Intelligence, Consideration, Thoughtfulness, Brain and Central Nervous Systems, Purity, Infinite Self, and Spiritual Innocence

Crystals, Stones, Minerals, and Precious Metals

Snow Quartz, Scolecite, Moonstone, Selenite, Arctic Quartz, White Calcite, Opal, and Ulexite

Sound Wave Frequency - Musical Note B

Vocal Toning Sound - "Aahng" or "Shhh"

Resonant Plant Frequencies

Rose, Chamomile, Helichrysum, White Lotus, Angelica Root, Spikenard, and Frankincense

Resonant Compliments

Spheres, Water Elements, White Feathers, Snowflakes, Starbursts, Diamonds, Phi, Rainbows, Sand, Salt, Orgone Generators, Flutes, Crystal Singing Bowls, Angels, Wings, Moon, White Lilies, and Jasmine

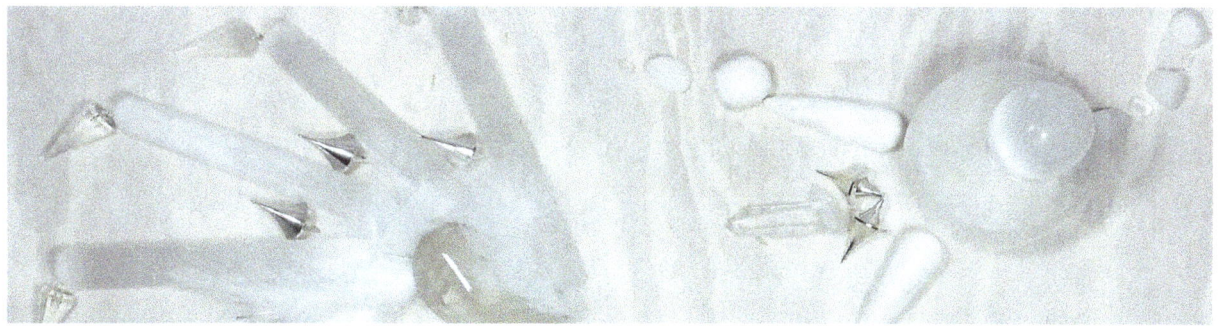

Black

Special note- Black works like a sponge, mopping up excessive negative and discordant energies, clearing away all that is not in a natural state of balance. Used alone it doesn't make for the best power generator or programming director. Used alone in a grid, the output will be very minimal unless it is Black Tourmaline, Arfvedsonite (aka Astrophyllite), Nuumite or Shungite. I strongly advise against using all black in a crystal alchemy grid. More is not always better. Too much black can feel depleting in general unless it is Shungite, Arfvedsonite (aka Astrophyllite) or Apache Tear. It's best used as an accent piece to keep the field stable and clear. Include some clear quartz to assist and consider some supportive orgone generators or metals or light and vibrant color frequencies. Use black as the field cleanser in moderation.

Governs

Absorbs Negative Energies, Unblocks Stuck Energy, Disperses Stagnant Energy, Neutralizes Radiation, Relief from Stress and Burdens, General Protection, Psychic Protection, Shielding, Cloaking, Secrecy, Depth, Retreat, Refuge, Untapped Potential Energy of the Great Void or Dark Matter, Stabilizes, and Accentuates Light

Crystals, Stones, Minerals, and Precious Metals

Black Tourmaline, Shungite, Black Onyx, Black Obsidian, Apache Tears, Nuumite, (Arfvedsonite aka Astrophyllite), Hematite, and Black Quartz

Sound Wave Frequency - Musical Note C and C#

Vocal Toning Sound - "Lahm"

Resonant Plant Frequencies

Sage, Pine, Frankincense, Cedarwood, Cypress, and Vetiver

Resonant Compliments

Orgone Generators, River Stones, Pine Branches, and Cones

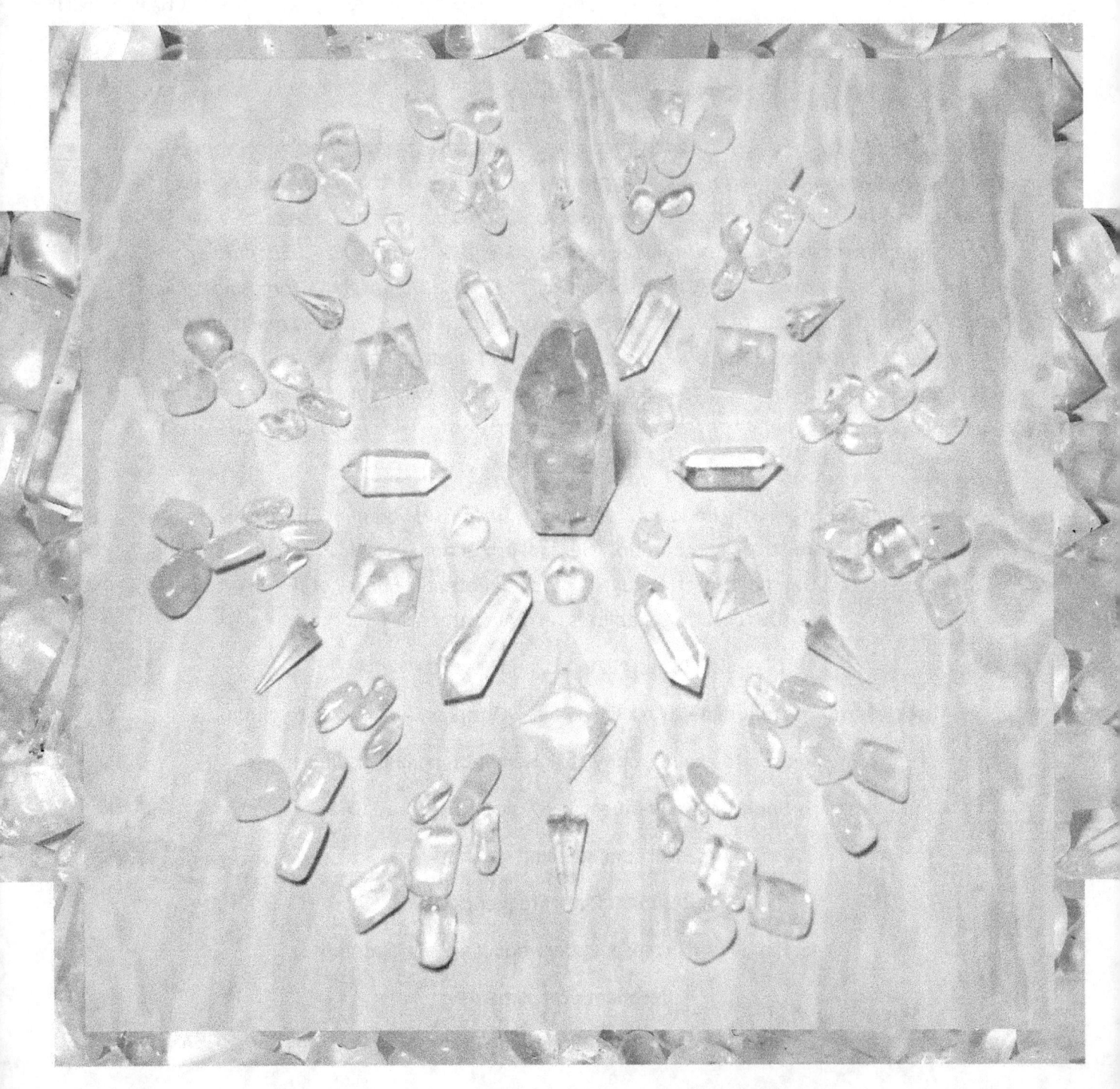

CHAPTER NINE

Clear

Clear crystals are the best for programming because they have no interfering mineral frequencies. Minerals are what give the color in stones and crystals. All minerals carry a unique governing frequency associated with their color cast.

Governs

Purity, Accelerated Energy, High Vibrations, Free Energy, Manifestation, Thought, Light, Information, Programming, Memory, Fluidity, Visibility, Transparency, Transitions, Sight, Perception, and portals to the multi-dimensions.

Crystals, Stones, Minerals, and Precious Metals

Clear Quartz, Herkimer Diamond, Fluorites, Apophyllite, Phenakite, Petalite, Lemurian Seed Crystal, Clear Calcite, Starbrary, and Selenite

Sound Wave Frequency - Musical Note A#

Vocal Toning Sound - "Ahng"

Resonant Plant Frequencies

Rose, Helichrysum, Blue Lotus, Lavender, Spikenard, and Frankincense

Resonant Compliments

Spheres, Spirals, Phi, Orgone Generators, Flutes, Crystal Singing Bowls, Water, Angels, Windows, Portals, and the Sun

CHAPTER NINE

Earth Tones

Governs

Humble Nature, Quiet Confidence, Self Assuredness, Reliability, Responsibility, Adaptability, Stress Reduction, Stability, Security, Integrity, Balance, and Support

Crystals, Stones, Minerals, and Precious Metals

Agates, Jaspers, Jades, Unakite, Golden Tiger Eye, Bronzite, Black Tourmaline, Black Onyx, Shungite, Arfvedsonite, Sardonyx, Petrified Wood, Bloodstone, Smokey Quartz, and All Metals

Sound Wave Frequency - Musical Note C# and C

Vocal Toning Sound - "Auhm" and "Lahm"

Resonant Plant Frequencies

Cedar Atlas, Pine, Balsam Fir, Vetiver, Patchouli, Juniper, and Angelica Root

Resonant Compliments

Leaves, Flowers, Driftwood, River Stones, Sand, Sea Salt, Pine Cones and Sprigs, Nuts, Sage, Seeds, Dried Fruit, Herbs, and Spices

Metals and Precious Metals

Frequency Field Stabilizers

Governs

Movement and Flow, Reflects Light, Stabilizes Energy, Draws in and Amplifies Energy

Precious Metal Gold

Gold has a very high frequency and governs cleansing and purification. Gold also governs the frequencies behind feelings of happiness, positivity, and optimism. It is a precious metal of general wellbeing in life. Because it can also house vast amounts of energy, it also governs abundance. Because it can handle running accelerated energy very well, it also governs energetic movement.

The sun and fire are natural compliments.

Resonant musical notes - E, F, and B

Precious Metal Silver

Silver is a healing precious metal in the medicinal sense. Silver helps to support and balance the emotional body, also making it ideal for enhancing intuitive abilities. Its energy is very soft and nurturing and so it works well as an amplifier and field stabilizer in crystal alchemy grids with the blue, green and pink color palettes.

The moon and water are natural compliments.

Resonant Musical Notes - C#, D, and A# and 432 Hz

Precious Metal Platinum

Platinum is a very high vibration precious metal and is protective of our spiritual being, integrity and energy field. Platinum works well to amplify and stabilize crystal alchemy grids. It has a beautiful synergy with white, clear, gold, silver, aqua or purple color palettes and any gratitude fields working with divinity, spirit, the angelics, celestial, and star beings, and the cosmos.

White Candles, Angels, and Crop Circles are Natural Compliments.

Resonant Musical Notes - Any sharp, and the frequency of 528 Hz

Pyrite

See Gold. Use as the "poor man's gold".

Resonant Musical Notes- D, D#, E, F, and B

Hematite

Magnetic Hematite has poles, making it ideal for balancing and stabilizing a crystal alchemy grid with multifaceted and complex intentions. Use it in black, silver, and earth tone color pallets.

The moon and water are natural compliments

Resonant Musical Notes - C, C#, and the Schumann Resonance

"Beauty attracts us, but if like an armed magnet it is pointed, beside, with gold and silver, it attracts with tenfold power." Jean Paul

Copper

Copper brings a lot of fire energy and amplification to a crystal alchemy grid. It's most appropriate when your affirmation includes transformation, because of the fire like heat it generates ethereally.

Fire and the sun are natural compliments

Resonant Musical Notes- C, D, and E

Most crystal shops carry metals like Pyrite, Hematite, and Copper. You can use authentic jewelry in your crystal alchemy grids and I do for bringing in the energies of the precious metals like Gold, Silver, Platinum and Rose Gold. There is another inexpensive way I found to bring in the energies of Silver and Gold when you want to use it in uniform multiples. At your local craft store, the jewelry making section will have packs of gold and silver plate or pure items. They make beautiful tiny accents to help to amplify and stabilize energy.

Non metallic items in the colors of precious metals will act more like a supportive governing color compliment instead of a field stabilizer or amplifier. You can add them as a symbolic compliment for support. Applying Gold, Silver or Copper leafing to a simple wood board or item is another gorgeous and unique way to bring the energy of authentic precious metals into your crystal alchemy grids.

About the Author

Tiari is excited to bring this body of inspiration to all who are drawn to deepen their empowerment and co-create with the support of the crystal wisdom keepers of Divine light. With the reconnection to her star family origins that happened on the magical north shore of Kauai in 1995, a natural interest in the developing planetary crystalline grid and healing with light and sound energy followed.

Tiari, an intuitive clairsentient, DNA-soul star and stargate activation key holder, has since spent decades studying, teaching and experimenting with energy healing in many forms related to creating coherent fields of light. She has covered vast areas of metaphysical study and is a Certified Master Instructor for the internationally practiced Integrated Energy Therapy, Sound Wave, and Crystal Alchemy energy attuning therapies and is certified in Pranic Energy Healing, Aromatherapy and Matrix Energetics. She also works with the Language of Light in vocal, written and hand signing light body activation codes.

After graduating from the Florida College of Natural Health, she opened and operated a successful wellness store and day spa business, near the crystal sand beaches of sunny Florida. Through this business, crystal healing and energy tools were a special part of the product lines and services offered. She developed many signature crystal and crystal sound wave energy attuning treatments for the day spa which are still being offered there today. It was there where she more deeply honed the intuitive skills of working with crystals from crystal stone massage and crystal singing bowl sound wave and alchemical crystal energy healing therapies along with chromotherapy, aromatherapy, gemstone elixirs and so much more.

Through the business, she rediscovered the arts of crystal grid making and began practicing and sharing the passion with others. To help get customers practicing the art of manifesting with crystal gridding at home, she even created her own crystal gridding kit with instruction guide and a package of templates for the store as they didn't yet exist in the marketplace at the time. They were soon to follow, and they then sold all other brands too!

And from out of those experiences in assisting others personally while sharing in her healing and accelerating energy practices, this book, which is the first of a series of more to come, was born. After selling the business to honor the call to move back to the paradise island of Kauai, she wanted to reach a broader audience through this upcoming book series on all the valuable ways to work with crystals in their daily life.

Tiari continues to practice and teach the energy healing arts while sharing her ascension activations, insights, and passion in the alchemy of crystal gridding through social media. For her, the crystals are very special to work with when co-creating. This is because they have shown her how they receive and hold the undistorted light from the Creator as they grow. "Their DNA actively vibrates with the keys and instructions for how to house the energy of our original innocence and purity, into the density of matter and it is magnificent," she exclaims!

For her, co-creating in dense matter is an on-going experiment in the realizations of what Divine creative intelligence has the potential to become. She shares, "We create things of beauty, things that inspire, things to appreciate. And, through those experiences we can feel the existence of something we cannot see, yet know is present within us and the joy of this being". She sees and feels within crystals a pulsation of powerful, undistorted, and uncorrupted light and sound codes of creation.

Tiari believes that human beings can act as crystals, stones, and minerals themselves

ABOUT THE AUTHOR

due to all the crystalline structures and minerals that the human body is created with. The difference to her is that the DNA within quartz is highly stable, and that of humans is not. The value of crystals, stones, and minerals to her is that they can act as pure extensions of the greater self.

She feels that the Law of One acknowledges that the whole of creation is one pulsating point of light. In her experience, she finds that we can affect matter within this point of light because we are a living part of it, as it is a living part of us. Crystals are more than just pretty objects to admire. They are our treasured, living and conscious companions too, she affirms.

Living in a lucid dream in Paradise and sharing from the heart....And So It Is........

Crystal Grid Alchemist. com

If you would like to enjoy more of Tiari's crystal alchemy grids, and other books, visit her web-site at www.crystalgridalchemist.com and Facebook page at Crystal Grid Alchemist.

Inspiration Photo at left - "Remote Plasma Light Healing Chamber" This grid utilizes a crystalline angelic place holder for the receiver and two crystalline angelic figurine place holders of the attending light body technicians. Plasma healing wand nanotechnology generates a plasma healing energy field and tubes of colored, liquid light to balance the light body. This was created for advanced energy healing and works on the same principles of remote energy healing.

Photo above - "Living the Dream Activation" Clear Quartz pyramid and double terminated wands for program directing and power generating, Apophyllite tips for heightening clarity of vision and being, Turquoise tumbleds and beads, Optical Orange Calcite and Aqua Aura double terminated points for affirmation support, copper for amplification and copper wire crafted Light Language activation codes.